GROWING UP BIRD:

OF ROOTS AND WINGS

A Collection of Family Stories

By

Kathryne Bird Belby

June, 2018

Cover photo: Soybean field Bird farm, Marcus, Iowa
July 2014

Dedicated to Mom and Dad ~

As time goes on, I understand you more

And thus, thank you from the bottom of my heart

Table of Contents

California, Here We Come!

Years ago, I was in the middle of planning our first big family vacation - a vacation that would take our family of six to the Black Hills and Mount Rushmore, Yellowstone and the Grand Tetons. My first call, in the days before the Internet, was to the National Park Service with whom I expected to quickly make reservations for lodging. When I learned that many of the sites in Yellowstone were already taken, I had a fleeting thought: maybe the trip wasn't worth the trouble. I still had to book flights, arrange for a rental van, and make other motel reservations. Anyway, how would our four kids do – ages 3 through 13 – stuck in a van, riding miles and miles between sights? Would they be squabbling the whole way? What if we hit a stretch of bad weather that dampened days and days of the trip?

And then I remembered my family's trip to California in 1964. It was the first bona fide vacation of my life and easily the most memorable.

Mom had planned the trip for months. We would travel from Iowa to San Francisco, then down the coast to Garden Grove, California to visit dad's brother Jim, his wife and five kids, then back to Iowa by way of Arizona. Pat, the youngest of us, was just two and a half, barely out of diapers and "travel ready." No matter that there were six kids between him and me (I was eleven); Mom was only thirty-five herself and had plenty of energy. She was determined that we take this trip. She had maps. She had brochures. She knew the places of interest all along interstate 80 from Iowa to San Francisco and beyond to Los Angeles. She spent her evenings poring over travel literature at the dining room table in preparation.

A lesser woman would have been daunted by the sheer statistics. Ten people, traveling in one vehicle for over 3,000 miles over a three-week period. Somehow, they must eat sixty- three times. Somehow, they must find lodging every night. And at least occasionally, they must have clean clothes.

Of course, we kids were oblivious to all this planning. We were just so excited we couldn't stand it. We had only been out of Iowa and our little town of Marcus (population 1300) to South Dakota and Minnesota. Did everyone in California have a suntan? Did they all skateboard? They probably surfed every day and sipped tropical juices through straws. I couldn't imagine us ever visiting a place as exotic as California.

"WE ARE GOING TO CALIFORNIA!" I wrote in all capitals on the cracked chalkboard in the basement; I felt as if we were going to another planet. To top it off, we were going in December and missing almost two weeks of school.

On the day we left, I remember circling the farmyard in our big white 1959 Chevy station wagon. Dad beeped the horn twice – his signature car communication mode – and proclaimed, almost like me: "California, here we come!" We all knew something momentous was beginning.

Dad and Mom manned the front seat, with maybe one kid in between and most times, the rest of us sprawled about the open back. Sometimes cars going by us on the interstate would slow down and we could see them point with their index fingers as they tried to count the moving heads. Dad would take both hands off the wheel for a split second and spread out all ten fingers in a dramatic census count. The other car would often honk as if to say "Thanks for the info!" and speed on.

Breakfast on the road was a quick bowl of Wheaties with brown sugar and maybe a few raisins. Lunch was a peanut butter or baloney sandwich and an apple. Mom had a cardboard box with the dining essentials carefully packed away: ten plastic bowls, ten plastic cups, ten spoons, ten forks and a few knives. Supper, in our motel, would be something Mom could fix on a hot plate, usually hot dogs and beans or soup. The expense log that mom and dad kept for the 21-day journey (with not one restaurant stop) showed the cost for food, lodging, gas, and entertainment for the entire almost three-week trip was $445.

We did get tired of the monotonous diet, but only one of us dared to complain – and just once.

"I'm sick of beans," Mike, who was just four, whined one night after we settled into a small motel room in California. We older kids gasped; we were all tired and cranky, but we knew better than to commit the Bird sin of complaining. To top it off, the usually agreeable and placid

3

Mike pushed his plastic bowl away and his beans slithered to the carpet. Before we knew what had happened, Dad had whacked Mike on the side of his head, and the jolt slammed his forehead right into the coffee table.

For whatever reason, Mom had planned that we visit a fancy department store in San Francisco a couple days later. So off we went, the ten of us, right on the heels of the bean incident, including Mike, who by now sported two vivid purple shiners.

Since it was Christmas time, Santa Claus was holding court in the toy section in the department store. He sat on a podium, surrounded by fake trees, cotton snow, and twinkly lights. We, in our warm overcoats and scarves (okay, mine was more like a Russian babushka), stuck out like sore thumbs in a crowd of trendy Californians. It just follows that Santa would be curious about our group, especially the small boy with the two black eyes.

"Hey, little boy," Santa beckoned to Mike, "would you like to come up and talk to Santa?"

Mike shrugged, but then dutifully made his way to the front.

"Why don't you sit on my lap?" Santa asked and Mike, ever obedient, did so.

"What's your name?" Santa asked.

Mike mumbled his name into Santa's beard, but Santa was having none of that.

"Can you say it louder into the microphone?" Santa prompted.

Mike leaned over and yelled his name, "MIKE!"

I cringed in the back.

"Are your mom and dad here?" Santa asked.

Mike, nodded, pointed them out, and the crowd focused on us just a little bit more, the oh-so-out of-place farmers from Iowa.

But Santa wasn't done. "What happened to your eyes, Mike?" he asked gently.

"My dad hit me," Mike answered. He had the hang of public speaking now and every single word came out loud and clear as he spoke into the microphone.

I suppose that even in the 1960s, Santa was so surprised that he didn't have time to check his reaction or change the subject. I mean, shouldn't he have followed that up with something like: "Ho-ho-ho! And what do you want for Christmas, little boy?"

No, instead, he asked the next natural thing: "And why did he do that, Mike?"

I cringed again. It seemed as if every tony shopper in that store had suddenly frozen, and pivoted toward Santa and Mike, poised there on the Christmas stage. The room fell totally silent.

Mike turned his big brown shiner ringed eyes out toward the crowd and took a deep breath. He would never whine again, and as a Bird, he certainly couldn't tell a lie either.

He turned back toward Santa, leaned over the microphone, and told the honest-to-goodness four-year-old truth.

"I spilled beans on the motel rug," he said simply and looked up at Santa.

And so, the beans-on-the-motel-rug story ends. We didn't stay for more honest explanations from Mike.

Mike never got to ask Santa for anything for Christmas, nor did anyone else. I don't even remember how we got out of that store. Perhaps we were on the first floor and ran out into the street. Perhaps we dashed down flights and flights of stairs. I only know that our exit was quick and final and that somehow, yes, someone remembered to gather up poor Mike on the way.

****

Finding a place to stay on our California trip was an interesting dilemma. The first night out, Dad stopped and innocently asked for a room for ten. Horrified, the clerk cited safety and fire regulations that prevented him from putting more than five people in a room. Dad was equally horrified that anyone would expect us to take TWO rooms and pay for them.

A bit wiser and farther down the road, Dad parked the car out of view of the front desk at the next motel and asked for a room for five people. We were able to get a room, although the clerk was quite concerned about that fifth person. Were we sure we didn't want a rollaway cot so that extra person could sleep comfortably? Oh no, Dad assured the clerk with a straight face; we will be just fine. Little did the clerk suspect that there would be five more people in the room, who would be sharing beds or sleeping on the floor in blankets.

From then on, our big decision was which five of us would be legitimate. The legitimate five could go in the office while Dad asked for a room. They could brazenly browse through brochures or go to the office for ice. The other five, who had driven around a bit more with Mom and then entered the motel room covertly, were more or less confined to quarters until checkout time the next morning.

Fortunately, 1964 was long before the days of blow dryers and hair conditioners, because with ten of us there was no way any one individual could use the bathroom for more than a couple minutes at a time. Courtesy of mom, the girls all had pixie cuts and the boys buzz cuts, which made hair care ultra-efficient. Washing our hair twice a week probably took about one hour for the whole family for the entire trip.

Since we were only able to use the bathroom for essential purposes, we devised our own methods for quasi-privacy. We all changed clothes at the same time in the same room: boys on one side, girls on the other. Everyone faced the nearest wall and at the count of "Go," we were on our honor to change without looking at anyone else. Once in a while a squeal of "Mom, he peeked at me!" would send the whole system into chaos. To the guilty ones, suffering the repercussions was worth a look.

Packing for the trip was streamlined and efficient, too. First, a pair of jeans was folded in half the long way. On top of this, we placed a matching shirt, folded in half, then a pair of underwear, and lastly, socks. This whole outfit-for-a-day was rolled up tightly, tied with baling twine, and placed in one of two large laundry bags, comprising all the luggage for the kids. We were each allowed three outfits, one of which we wore.

In the seatbelt-less car, we kids sprawled out in the open back, lying on the laundry bag pillows and passing the time by playing cards and picking on each other. We would be good for only so long and then sibling hazing would start. "She looked at me!" "Get a new face!" Mom and Dad would drive along, ignoring us as long as possible. Then, suddenly, without warning, Dad's long arm of the law would make a sweep of the back of the station wagon. Instantly, everyone would be out of reach, plastered along the back window. A close call like that was enough to make us get along for at least another half hour.

Day after day of baloney sandwiches, beans, and soup and not too much physical activity took its toll on our digestive systems. And traveling in December meant all the windows were up, making conditions just right for really getting even if you happened to be angry at someone. You could actually choose to sit right next to your archenemy, make civil conversation until he forgot about your recent fight and then pass gas, just as you broke into bawdy laughter. The other kids, most of whom had been innocently playing card games, would scream "Hold your cards!" as they rolled down all the car windows at once for fresh air. "Hold your cards" is still an inside family joke.

Since I was eleven and the oldest, I probably remember more about the actual sightseeing on the trip than anyone else. The Mormon Tabernacle, the salt flats of Utah, the greenness of Sacramento seen in the same day as the snowy Donner Pass, the Golden Gate Bridge and park, the San Francisco zoo, Lombard Street, Alcatraz, Muir Woods with the giant redwoods, Knott's Berry Farm, the Pacific Ocean, and yes, Disneyland. Even if our little black and white photos couldn't capture the grandeur of those faraway places, all those sights were forever etched in my eleven-year-old head.

And I have a slant on them the average traveler would never experience. In Salt Lake City, the tour guide in the Mormon Tabernacle eyed the ten of us clad in bulky winter coats and boots (I in a somber black scarf) and remarked to the group, "This family here could be a typical Mormon family."

"Oh, no, we're Catholic!" Mom quickly set him straight.

I remember Dad negotiating Donner Pass in a blizzard (he stopped and put chains on our tires at the base), while Mom regaled us with the tale of the unfortunate Mr. Donner and his party who were stuck on that very mountain in the 1840s and resorted to cannibalism to survive. I remember little about the animals in the San Francisco zoo, but I do remember fighting over who got to use the "zookey", a red plastic key in the shape of an elephant that turned on an automatic recording at each animal exhibit. I also remember accidentally going up Lombard Street, the "Crookedest Street in the World," the wrong way in our trusty station wagon as Mom and Dad argued about whose fault it was.

And of course, there was the high-level conference that we kids had in Disneyland to determine which ONE ride we were all going to do - together. At the time, admission to the park was free and you paid for each ride individually. Mom and Dad agreed that we could do one ride out of the whole park, with the caveat that we all had to agree on the same ride. Much to Tom and Jeff's chagrin, a majority of us picked the monorail, which slid very slowly, and boringly, around the park on an elevated rail.

Bird Cousins ~ Garden Grove, California
December 1964

Front row: Tom, David*, Mike, Joe, Pat, Laurie*
Middle: Jeff, Mary, Debbie*
Back: Kathy, Paula* holding baby Diane, Jane.
* indicates cousins, children of Jim and Bev Bird

We spent Christmas with our Uncle Jim Bird, his wife Bev, and our first cousins in Garden Grove, who showed us how to play Rook, lived in a ranch style house, had TVs in their bedrooms, and yes, taught some of us how to skateboard. Amazingly, all ten of us stayed with them in the same house for a week.

Of course, years later, I went on to plan my own family's trip out West. Mom had sparked a love of travel in me and I wanted to pass on that love to my kids. I wanted them to see the world outside of NJ, just as Mom had worked so hard to show us the incredible sights beyond our Iowa farm. I say Mom, because although Dad was the ultimate authority once the trip was in motion, it was Mom who dreamed the idea, researched the sightseeing, and organized the logistics. It was Mom, with her voracious reading and love of history, who gave us an appreciation of the stories and scenery of our country, and organized a second trip to Washington, D.C. a few years later.

Unwittingly, and somewhat sadly, it was through Mom's very efforts to educate us - through books, travel, and experiences – that most of us found ourselves settling quite a distance from our childhood home. She had done her job well; she had ignited our curiosity. But once kindled, she could not hold us back.

Had Mom guessed the bittersweet, unintended consequences of exposing us to the world beyond Marcus, would she have changed the way she raised us? For only Pat stayed close by and took over the family farm. The rest of us, who landed in Ames, Iowa; Manhattan, Kansas; Chicago; Minneapolis; Denver, Colorado; and New Jersey, are distant members of a once close tribe, scattered across the very country Mom worked so hard to show us.

Seal Rock, San Francisco, Dec 1964

Bottom row: Mike, Pat, Joe, Mary
Back row: Jeff, Tom, Dad, Jane, Mom, Kathy

Low Tech Down Time

Christmas 1963 with low tech presents:
Front row: Pat & Mike unknown presents
Second row: Joe with GI Joe, Mary with medicine kit, Jane
with microscope
Jeff with game, Tom unknown present, Kathy with five-
year diary

Low Tech Down Time

When our assigned work on the farm or in the house was finished, we generally made ourselves scarce. There may have been a few times when I dared to sit on the couch and read in sight of mom when my chores were done. But I quickly learned that an idle-appearing kid not only annoyed her but was also grist for her chore list.

"Hey," she might say on her way through the living room where I was reading, "are the little boys (Joe, Mike, and Pat) done playing in the sand box? I'm just wondering if they put the screen over it so the cats can't poop in it?"

She had a point. The cats might be semi-wild things that lived their furtive lives in the shadows of the barn, but somehow they could mysteriously and quickly find their way to an unattended sand box to do their business.

Still, cats aside, if I was reading my head was somewhere else.

"I don't know," I'd murmur. Right at that moment, Pa Ingalls was at the window of the Little House in the Big Woods. It was dark and he had Laura in his arms so she could see the wolves howling in the woods. There were two of them and their eyes were yellow.

"Well, I just hate those damn dirty cats digging in the same sand the boys play in," Mom would say, setting up the ironing board in the dining room about ten feet from me.

"Uh-huh," I'd say. I was glad that Laura, and Mary, and Ma weren't alone in their cabin and that Pa was back from town.

Mom would spread one of dad's blue work shirts over the ironing board and sprinkle it with water, the iron hissing and spitting as she mashed it back and forth over the damp cotton.

"I can see that the boys out there on the swings now," she'd say, glancing out the window. "Guess they aren't playing in the sandbox anymore."

"Guess not," I'd murmur. The wolves had quieted for now and Pa was playing his fiddle by the fireplace.

She got out a second shirt, sprinkled it with water, too, laid one sleeve on the ironing board, and flattened it with hot authority.

"Those damn cats know just when the sand box is uncovered," she said, going after the second sleeve in rapid succession.

"Yes," I'd say. It was snowing now at the Little House in the Big Woods, but the Ingalls family was safe and warm inside, dancing to Pa's music.

Mom spread out the collar of Dad's shirt next, and mashed those wrinkles out, too.

"You know the little boys could get worms if they play in the sand with cat poop," she remarked.

"Yeah," I said. Laura climbed into the bed she shared with Mary. She was getting so sleepy what with the peaceful snow outside, the warm fireplace, Pa home from town, and the wolves finally quiet in the woods. She snuggled next to Mary and watched the shadows Pa made on the cabin wall as he put his fiddle away.

15

"Wonder if those cats are in the sandbox now?" Mom mused. She was wrapping up the second shirt, her iron fairly flying over the broad expanse of its back.

"Dunno," I said. I turned the page to the next chapter of the Little House in the Big Woods.

Mom got a third shirt out of the laundry basket and paused. "Say," she said, pretending the thought had just occurred to her, "why don't you go out there and check to see if the boys put that screen over the sandbox?"

I closed my book. I would have to put the Ingalls family on hold. To mom's mind, this was an emergency. Far as she knew, the barn cats might be out there right now, cavorting and pooping in their very own tractor tire litter sandbox.

"Okay," I said begrudgingly and started towards the door.

"While you're out there, get the sheets in from the line," she said. "Bring the laundry basket with you."

I picked up the basket without a word.

"And could you check to see if there are a couple ripe tomatoes for supper?"

"Okay," I said, opening the screen door. I heaved a big sigh.

At that point she sometimes realized that she was heaping chore upon chore. Even so, she couldn't help herself.

"And while you're at it," she might laugh, "stick a broom up your ass and sweep on your way out."

****

And so, knowing we would get a job to do if we just hung around in plain sight of Mom, we quickly learned to occupy ourselves with activities when our work was done. With eight siblings, almost all of us close enough to be Irish twins, there was always something to do and someone to do it with.

There were traditional kid activities, like riding bikes. Early on, courtesy of farm auctions, we each had something to ride: no fancy gears or narrow speed enhancing tires for us. Later on, the younger kids got Schwinn bikes for Christmas, but before that, our bikes were all sizes of multi-colored or sometimes-rusted contraptions with big fat seats and wide tires that were actually better for the loose gravel country roads. Not one bike could be claimed by any one kid; the only bike we fought over was the one with the cool banana seat.

We older kids taught the younger ones to ride, running alongside as they pumped furiously down the lane.

"Peddle, peddle, peddle!" we'd yell. "Keep peddling!"

They'd stay upright just until it dawned on them that they were actually riding a bike solo, just until that very thought paralyzed their uncertain legs, just until the bike coasted down the slight incline into the big yard, just until they made a slow circle with the little momentum they had gathered, until both bike and rider toppled unceremoniously into the dust.

"You're not hurt!" we older kids would yell before the new biker could cry, egging the would-be rider to get up, dust off the grime, and try again.

It took little encouragement, for the allure of bike freedom called to us all. On a bike, we could go almost anywhere. First, we stayed on the flat packed earth of the big yard, practicing wide turns and getting the feel of brakes. Then we ventured "up the hill," on a lane with slight rise towards the well in the middle of the farm. Next, we were allowed to ride a half-mile on the gravel road to get the mail with an older buddy. We rode back and forth to our neighbors' houses to play and then graduated to doing the section, a four-mile square on which our house sat. Eventually, we all made the trek to town and back (13 miles of flat easy riding).

When we tired of riding bikes, there were always games to play outside. The back-porch closet held heaps of sports equipment: jump ropes, badminton racquets and nets, volleyballs, a croquet set, bats, softballs, baseballs, mitts, and basketballs. With only one other person, you could get some kind of competition going; with four, a team game. My closest rival was Jane, who bested me in almost every contest, from racing to shooting hoops to smacking a softball. No matter, I was both up to play anything and eternally optimistic that I might eventually beat her. Besides any kind of game was better than being a house lackey for mom!

The farm also provided us with plenty of other opportunities for creative games. In the grove - the stand of trees to the west - there was a weather beaten empty house, once lodging for hired help. Gray and dilapidated, there was nothing further we could damage in it, for the floors had long ago lost their finish, and most of the windows were gone. It was the perfect spot in which to play house – in a real house-sized house. We had some old dresses from our Grandma Seuntjens and I remember always vying for the role of mother, which I could usually boss my way into. We made mud pies out of the thick loamy Iowa soil and set them on the windowsills to bake/dry. We played hide and seek there, and sometimes brought down buckets of water from the well pump, washing the floor by sloshing it, and of course, getting each other wet in the process.

The grove was full of big tall weeds and grass and when we tired of playing in the house, we made mazes in the vegetation and played tag. We formed a secret club in that grove, so secret that in order to be initiated, you needed to drink a potion that we concocted by combining leftover chemicals from tin containers that Dad had discarded on the junk pile. Fortunately, one small sip was enough to ensure a lifelong membership in the nameless club- probably just one small sip away from being actually poisoned!

We invented other games, too, such as gymnastics in the hayloft. Our balance beam was a support beam that ran across the expanse of the barn and was actually about as wide as a real balance beam. We'd practice ten feet or so above the hay bales, arms out wide, falling to safety when one of our siblings purposely broke our concentration. We swung on the rope that was originally used to pull up bales by a pulley or went hand over hand along its length as far as we were able.

Miraculously, besides not being poisoned, no one was hurt too badly or broke any limbs in our roughhouse playing. My worst injury was a puncture wound from a tine on the manure loader, which was parked by a tree from which hung an inviting chain. I could grab that chain, I envisioned, and swinging hard, land right in the manure loader bucket. Unfortunately, I miscalculated and impaled my calf on a manure-covered spike, which resulted in one of the rare visits (besides for vaccines) to see Dr. Joynt in Marcus. Dr. Joynt's ancient and tiny nurse, Cora – her white braids wrapped around her head - met Mom and me at the top of the long dark stairs leading to Dr. Joynt's office. Cora cleaned my manure loader wound; I was given a shot of something (maybe two shots: hopefully tetanus and penicillin!) and sent on my way, with only a silvery half-moon scar on my calf to show for it. Once Tom narrowly escaped injury when Mom accidentally rode over his leg with the pickup (nothing broken!), and Jane cracked her nose climbing on a dresser stacked on another, which fell over on her face. But other than that, our rambunctious play left us remarkably unscathed.

Presents at Christmas were generally low key. Three gifts were the norm: one practical, like pajamas; one educational – a chemistry set; and one fun - GI Joe or a doll. But one year, Santa went big and got the whole family a ping-pong table. Somehow, we squeezed it into our basement under the clotheslines, between the galvanized rinsing tubs and the wall of the fruit room. We set up brackets and held family tournaments (with Dad or Jane usually winning). We roller skated under the table when we weren't playing ping-pong, scrunching up our bodies to coast under it, gathering up speed by circling around the basement steps.

In the dead of winter, we could only play so much ping-pong, cards (hearts, spades, rummy, crazy eights, Rook, Old Maid), Monopoly, or checkers before we got restless, which called for a game of basketball outside. If the snow was manageable, we'd shovel down to the bare earth by the barn, and then sweep it clean with a broom, just so we could play. Sometimes, before we managed to get outside, the boys would get antsy and pick at each other until a fight ensued. This might last just a short time until Dad came in and ordered:

"Okay, that's enough. Go outside and run around the house fifteen times."

It might be twenty degrees or zero or minus twenty, but no one argued with dad. Instantly, the boys would separate, go into the basement, and bundle up to do their obligatory laps.

Fortunately for me (unlike the boys), I didn't have to do much in the way of outside chores in the winter – only watering the chickens or getting the eggs from the henhouse. So playing outside in the snow was more of a treat – making forts and snowmen. But I especially liked taking walks along the road at night after a snowfall – the packed snow squeaking under my boots and the moon high and white. Once I walked with Mary after a blizzard that dumped so much snow in northwest Iowa that Army tanks had to come and open the roads. The road was lined with eight-foot high piles of snow, creating a white half tunnel that absorbed all sound except for our crunching footfalls and our voices, muffled by scarves. For a while, in that eerily windless night with not a car or house in sight, we pretended that we were explorers in a snowy far off land of sharp moon shadows, the only humans around. When we tired of that, we talked of everything sisters do, our fingers and toes numb, our limbs bundled in layers, cocooned and safe on that road in the still white night.

****

Being one of eight siblings was not all that unusual in the Iowa of the 1960s. In fact, most of our friends from Holy Name grade school were also from big families. Our neighbors, the Seggermans, had ten children one of whom was my friend, Diane. Combined, our families made two perfect softball teams and so most Sunday evenings we'd get together to play. Dad and Bob (the Seggerman's father) would pitch and catch and monitor the score so that we nearly always ended up in a tie or something close to it. If one of the little ones was up to bat and had already missed two times, on the third miss, Bob would say, "Two and a half!" and let them try again...and again...until they finally made contact with the ball. You were almost always guaranteed to score unless your team was far ahead, in which case, one of the dads - who called the plays - might determine you were inexplicably out. You hadn't really touched home plate, they'd say, or maddeningly, in a burst of speed they'd actually tag you out, something they'd been unable to do to anyone else.

Afterwards, there would be more games – the kids might do volleyball, badminton, kick the can, or freeze tag while the parents played pinochle over a glass of Pabst beer. To wind the night down, we'd sit on the south porch swing and munch on popcorn straight out of a big enamel dishpan, until everything but a few buttery old maids were left at the bottom.

****

Although the Bird-Seggerman softball games were non-competitive, nearly every other game we played among ourselves was a contest to see who was stronger or faster. Any activity could be turned into a competition or a dare: finishing chores, racing to the mailbox, eating the most donuts, making the most free throws in a row, standing on your head the longest, jumping rope without missing a beat. Anything.

One Christmas Eve after we had opened our presents, we sat around the dining room table, playing some kind of game and snacking. There was a tub of Mom's Christmas cookies on the table and fudge and divinity and popcorn balls and candy canes and...a bowl of oranges. We rarely had oranges and they didn't interest us that much except that these oranges were so small (tangerines?) that Joe mused he could probably swallow one whole.

"Betcha can't," we chorused.

"Bet I can," Joe said.

"No way," we baited him. "Betcha can't!"

"Well, I'd have to take the skin off," he hedged.

"So take the skin off," one of us allowed. "Dare you – take the skin off then – and swallow it whole."

"Watch this," he said, his ever-confident voice wavering just a little. He took the skin off with great aplomb and with all eyes on him, popped the whole thing into his mouth and gulped.

As I remember it, all chatter died away. The orange appeared to slide into his throat, but there it lodged, tight as a cork in a bottle. Joe, never one to give up, kept trying to swallow. And still we watched him, as his face turned red, as he became unable to speak, as he took the dare to its extreme.

"He looks like he's choking," someone said.

"I think maybe he is," another sibling agreed. Joe gulped and strained and swallowed some more.

"Are you choking?" we finally asked, a few years before the famous doctor would coin the phrase.

Joe gasped and nodded. Not knowing what else to do, someone slapped him on the back and the whole slimy thing popped out.

Little did we realize that we had just performed a near perfect sequence of the as-yet-to-be-discovered Heimlich maneuver. We could have become famous, traveling around the country demonstrating that simple first aid technique – the Bird maneuver – but the thought never occurred to us. All we knew was that Joe was okay, but more importantly - in the end - he had lost the dare.

****

And so, we learned to make ourselves scarce when our work was done. For me, reading became the perfect escape. Through books, I followed Laura Ingalls Wilder back in time to the previous century and then <u>Mara, Daughter of the Nile</u> into ancient Egypt. I traveled the

United States with Lois Lenski, who wrote regional books about real kids: <u>Bayou Suzette</u>, <u>Strawberry Girl</u>, <u>Blue Ridge Billy</u>, <u>Corn Farm Boy</u>. I sat with Jo and Beth and Amy and Meg in <u>Little Women</u> and wondered what Massachusetts was like. I read <u>Anne of Green Gables</u> and tried to picture Prince Edward Island. I lost myself in an alternate world in Madeline L'Engle's <u>A Wrinkle in Time</u>.

Mom encouraged our reading habits with biweekly Saturday trips to the Marcus library (right after Confession!), toting our mother lode of reading material back and forth in a large cardboard apple box. This was one area of our lives in which we weren't limited; we could check out as many books as we wanted. When they were in the primary grades, the Tom and Jeff might disappear into the easy reader section, while Jane and I looked through middle school books. Once she made sure the little ones were occupied with picture books (or being watched), Mom herself would sneak to the periodical section and grab the latest *Saturday Evening Post, Life,* or *Look* magazines. After a half hour or so, we would bring our selections to the front desk where Mrs. Mossman, her thin veined hands shaking ever so slightly, would stamp the cards for a date two weeks in the future.

To supplement our library reading, the *Sioux City Journal,* the Catholic diocesan paper *The Globe,* the *Wallace's Farmer,* and *Nursing* were delivered to our house. The *Journal* would be quickly scanned at dinner – the midday meal – for important regional news, like Briar Cliff going coed or Iowa Beef Packers opening a plant just across the river from Sioux City. The other publications would be considered after supper, when Mom would often sit for the first time all day and quietly fall asleep, an illustration of a new syringe or a photo of the bishop at a local confirmation open on her lap.

Through reading, we became curious about other areas of the country and the world. What would it be like to live in a city or along a coast? What would it be like to speak another language? We learned about occupations other than farming. What would it be like if our father worked in an office? What would it be like to be an explorer? A detective? A doctor? A writer? Through books my imagination was unleashed; I was transported through barriers of time and space.

Beyond travel, Mom was opening us up to a world outside of Marcus. Unwittingly, was she fostering our flight from home? Did stimulating our curiosity cause some of us to end up at a distance far beyond what she had ever considered?

None of us thought of that at the time. I know only that when I wasn't busy, I began burying myself in books.

Just not in the living room, in full view of Mom!

Faith

Kathy (2nd grade), Principal Sister Mary Joselita,
Jane (1st grade), and Sister Mary
Bryan Joseph from Holy Name grade school
during visit to farm to solicit donation for a new convent
1961

Faith

"Who is God?" Sister Mary Bryan Joseph asked.
I got out of my seat, stood by my desk, and answered in a complete sentence: "God is the Supreme Being who made all things." I was in the first grade and catechism– which Sister Mary Bryan Joseph said was the most important subject - was the first order of the day. She had taught us that God knows all things and sees all things. Could He see us right now in our little Holy Name grade school, tucked away in Marcus, Iowa?

There were sixty of us in that one classroom, 30 first graders and 30 second graders, yet somehow that young nun managed to make the concept of God start to take shape for me. He was everywhere, surrounded by angels, watching my every move and I'd better be good. I didn't question Sister Mary Bryan Joseph about anything: math, phonics, reading, spelling, or penmanship, and that included religion, too. At six years old, if any adult, much less a nun, told me something, I assumed it was true and religion was no different.

And so, I learned about faith – about being Catholic – first by memorization. We are made in the image and likeness of God: to know Him, to love Him, and to serve Him in this world and to be happy with Him in the next. There are three persons in the Trinity: Father, Son, and Holy Ghost. A sacrament is an outward sign instituted by Christ to give grace. There are seven sacraments and they are: Baptism, Penance, Holy Eucharist, Confirmation, Matrimony, Holy Orders, and Extreme Unction...

These rote answers meant little to me at first, but gradually they became a framework on which to hang more information and more complicated concepts. How were we expected to serve God? What happened to us when we were baptized? How would I actually become a "soldier of Jesus Christ" during Confirmation?

Each year built on the last. In second grade we learned about saints: real bona fide people whom we were named after and could pray to for help. No Halloween for us; instead, we dressed up like our namesakes and wore our costumes to Mass on All Saints' Day. I was St. Catherine of Siena, who was smart and some kind of a writer. There was a picture of her on one of the stained-glass windows in Holy Name, in a two-toned blue veil and robe, holding a palm frond made into a pen of sorts, which mom somehow had time to dutifully copy. Next, after spending a few weeks on sin, and hoping that all mine were venial, I slipped into the dark confessional and was relieved to be absolved by Father O'Reilly. (After all, part of forgiveness hinged on the resolution that I would never commit the offense again and I couldn't be sure that I would never hit Jane or Tom for all of eternity!) Then on December 8th, on the Feast of the Immaculate Conception, shivering in my flimsy white dress and tiny anklets, I made my First Communion along with my classmates. I hoped to feel something seismic with each sacrament: a shift to a holier girl who would never fight or never talk back to her mother again. A girl so cleansed from confession and so filled with the Eucharist, that those pesky venial sins would never come on her radar again.

When that didn't happen, I kept the secret deep inside. Maybe I would just have to keep trying. What else to do when you are eight? Because we were human – the nuns said - we would need to work at it for the rest of our lives; hence, the need for frequent confession, communion, and Mass; all of which would give us grace. We were building up a storehouse of sorts, a bank of goodness to draw on for those dark times.

And build up a bank, we did. At Holy Name, we went to Mass three times a week - every Monday, Wednesday, and Friday - and said a rosary afterwards on each of those days to add to our cache of grace. We girls covered our heads with scarves or chapel veils, and if we had neglected to bring either of those, a folded Kleenex secured with a bobby pin sufficed. Going to Mass shortened recess on those days by a good thirty minutes, but no one dared complain. Going to school at Holy Name provided a very solid introduction to the Catholic faith; whether we chose to follow it or not was up to us.

At home, Mom and Dad didn't talk about faith much and they didn't pray aloud extemporaneously. I never heard them ask God for rain or ask for the rain to stop. I never heard them pray that the price of corn, soybeans, cattle, or hogs would go up. I never heard them pray aloud for a sick relative or neighbor. I don't think they prayed that we got good grades. I never heard them pray for the president or the country. I never even heard them pray for each other.

Yet, I think their seeming reticence in talking about faith had more to do with their mode of rarely talking about anything intangible, than lack of faith itself. They simply didn't talk much about feelings. I never heard Mom or Dad say they were sad or happy, stressed or calm, excited or just plain tired of everything. In general, they felt that you should make the most of whatever was handed to you: rain or not, low prices or high prices, sickness or health. God was present, but this was life and you could not expect it would always go your way. I'm thinking they didn't blame God for setbacks or expect Him to work miracles just for them. They dealt with life as it was. God helps those who help themselves, Mom and Dad allowed, as they raised eight of us on their share of a tenant farmer's income: a meager half of what the sale of their crops earned.

Did they pray in the silence of their hearts? Did they each pray to God in their own way?

"Jesus God, let it rain soon."

"God, let this baby be okay."

"Help me find patience."

I can't be certain, but I'd lay odds they did.

What they DID do is to take us to Mass every Sunday, most times the ten of us at once, squirming babies and all. We sat on the left-hand side of the church about ten rows back from the statue of Mary and we took up two pews. As I remember, we were always on time, and limited as funds were, we had actual church clothes: better shoes than play shoes, dress pants (not jeans) for the boys, hats and white gloves for the girls in summer. We listened to Father O'Reilly's short and pointed sermons, chatted with neighbors afterwards, and stopped at Grandma Bird's for toast and jam when Mass was over. In the afternoon, we visited relatives or neighbors. There you have it – a wrap for Sunday: no factoring in midget football, or wrestling practice, or traveling soccer. And despite the demanding nature of running a farm, as a rule, we did very little work on Sunday.

Mom and Dad did not go on mission trips and I'm thinking they did not have extra money to send to charities, besides the church. They lived by Mom's pronouncement that God wanted you to take care of your own family first and not be "running around with a wheel up your ass." Still, when someone died, she could and would whip up a cake or pie and drop it off almost before the funeral home picked up the body. They helped paint the school. They got up early and took the boys in to serve their rotations of the 7 a.m. Mass on Tuesdays or Thursdays and we girls went along to warble hymns from the choir loft. They took us to confession once a month – and I repeated those irksome never-resolved sins: talking back to my mother and fighting with my brothers and sisters. They said night prayers with us when we were little. We said grace before every meal, three times a day, 365 days a year.

Each year, Mom took us to May Crowning – a devotion to Mary that took place on a weeknight during one of the busiest times on the farm. We girls wore our best dresses and headbands of fake flowers, while the boys dressed in white shirts and ties. We pulled out all the Marian stops, singing every Mary song known to the nuns and decorated the church with fragrant purple lilacs.

Ready for May Crowning, 1961 ~ Tom, Jane, and Kathy

And Mom – like all the other Moms I knew - belonged to the Guild, a group of Holy Name women who met once a month to listen to an inspirational speaker. The Guild ladies were also each assigned to a month of the year and tasked with helping for all the funeral dinners that month. Mom always hoped for a light month – and was quietly relieved when an expected death fell just before the first or after the thirty-first of her month. Still, whenever the passing landed solidly within her assigned time, she went and worked with her guild sisters. Side by side, they unfolded metal chairs and set them up at the long paper covered tables. They made huge urns of coffee. They set out individual pieces of made-from-scratch fruit pies and cakes. They whipped up mashed potatoes, carved up thick slices of ham, cooked Del Monte green beans and served them up to the grieving families of the bereaved. When the last of the funeral goers had left, when the last story had been told ("I remember when your folks bought that 80 acres southwest of town." "Your dad was quite the baseball player in high school." "That was about the time we had that terrible blizzard." "Your aunt was quite the classy dresser when she went out."), when the helpers had had a bite to eat themselves, they washed the platters and pans, wiped down the counters and stoves, and put away everything, leaving the kitchen ever at the ready for the next end of life event.

As I matured, I began to put it all together. Right there in that little town I had seen the Corporal and Spiritual Works of Mercy:

Feed the hungry

Give drink to the thirsty

Visit the sick

Bury the dead

Comfort the sorrowful

Pray for the living and the dead

In essence, the Guild ladies had hit quite a few of them – all in one fell swoop.

And so, I grew up with that solid foundation of faith in place. I attended Holy Name all through grade school (as did all my younger siblings, until it was shuttered in 1972) and went to religious classes on Sundays after that – all the way through high school – where fittingly, as sort of a send-off, we spent our senior year learning about marriage.

Once we went away to college, mom and dad never asked us if we were going to church or practicing our faith. This silence surrounding our Catholicism had a kind of "don't ask, don't tell" feel to it. I don't think any of us wanted to disappoint mom and dad and so we either kept the faith…or pretended we were doing so when they visited us. This was one area where we did not openly defy them; our silence on the matters of religion was sometimes more a sign of respect than agreement.

Yet, my own faith deepened in Briar Cliff, a small Catholic college in Sioux City. We had lively Masses with moving music and dynamic homilies directed towards twenty-somethings. We had nuns teaching some of the science classes and priests teaching theology and a chaplain who was readily available for questions in his office. And in the same way that mom and dad, classmates, relatives, neighbors, my teacher nuns, and even Father O'Reilly surrounded me with Catholicism as a kid, the students at Briar Cliff rounded out a faith supported milieu. We did "normal" college stuff at the time: we got fake IDs and went to South Dakota so we could drink underage; we went to parties; we sometimes stayed out too late to be on top of our game for class the next day, but in a sense, since most of the kids around me were Catholic, they made it easier to "keep the faith."

Where some might have felt this environment stifling and more of the same, I was comforted and nourished by it. I found it a safe place to figure out deeper spiritual questions as I matured.

Did I ever question my faith? Sure. Did I even learn about or investigate other faiths? Sure. But in the end, I became one of those rare Catholics who never left their faith. The Church, with all its rituals, its rich heritage, its music, its incense, its rote yet comforting prayers – and its problems – centers me. It is part of who I am.

Not all of my siblings practice Catholicism, but Mom and Dad provided a solid spiritual base from which we were free to springboard. We left home knowing Christ. We had a working knowledge of the commandments and had watched Mom and Dad try to live by them. Many of us have chosen work in the service of others, and I believe, that if we were to dig deep inside ourselves, each of us would eventually discover that a tiny seed of faith, planted long ago by our Catholic upbringing, has in large part shaped the way we live.

Mom and Dad practiced their faith until the end of their lives. Nearing retirement age, they moved into town and were happy to find a house just across the street from Holy Name. At least once a week they attended daily Mass, afterwards combining fellowship and faith with coffee and breakfast at the Big Booth. Fittingly, their funerals were at the same church that had seen them through life's ups and downs; their Masses celebrated by a priest who knew them well.

Of Dad, Father Murphy said at his funeral (paraphrasing): "Bill was of a generation of young men who came back to this area after WWII, determined to put that experience behind him. He did it, like many others, by working hard at being a good father, husband, and farmer." In this simple statement, Father Murphy publicly acknowledged the demons of war that seemed to bother Dad more at the end of his life (especially his experiences at Iwo Jima), yet at the same time he paid tribute to a life well lived.

Mom lived a full year after Dad, her world growing smaller and smaller with the increasing demands on her body for enough oxygen. Yet she could and did motor across the street in her scooter, oxygen in tow, take the elevator, and continue going to Mass.

As much as she retained every bit of mental acuity until the last flicker of life left her, she held on to her faith. On the night of her death, six of us took turns sitting at her bedside. A few hours before she died, Mary and I found ourselves in that darkened room. The oxygen concentrator hummed and clicked in the background. Mom's breathing became less regular. A tsunami of emotions coursed inside me: my mother was leaving me. The woman who had borne me, fed me, clothed me, educated me, prodded me, guided me, and sometimes badgered me- but ultimately loved me and my siblings unequivocally -would be dead in a very short time. Although she was conscious, she was too weak to converse. In truth, there were no words for that moment anyway. Thank you would not cover it. I owe my life to you – decidedly too unBirdlike. I love you – already said and implicitly understood.

What to do? How to endure the next hard hour or perhaps even minutes? And then, although I have no idea how it came about, suddenly Mary and I began saying the rosary. Mom followed along, eyes closed, lips moving in tandem with the words we said aloud. Her fingers moved along the beads, the skin on her hands paper thin at the end of her life. I had no problem beginning with the Apostle's Creed, the Glory Be, and the three introductory Hail Marys of the iconic Catholic devotion.

But next came the decades themselves. It was a Monday and I couldn't remember which mysteries went with Monday, but I knew I didn't want to say the sorrowful mysteries on the night of Mom's death.

"The first joyous mystery," I decided. "The Annunciation." And the three of us prayed our way through the first decade.

Just in time, I remembered that the Visitation came next and we made it through decade two. Using logic, we segued into the third decade – the Birth of Christ - without too much difficulty. But closing in on the last few Hail Marys of decade three, I drew a blank.

"The fourth joyous mystery," I began and my voice faltered. I looked at Mary for help and she shook her head.

"The fourth joyous mystery…." I repeated.

And then, like phoenix rising from ashes, mom spoke. She raised her hands above her head, rosary beads draped between thumbs, drew one of her last breaths and said:

"The Presentation in the Temple."

****

A few days later, the very same Father Murphy presided over Mom's funeral. Though her death was expected and I thought I had prepared myself for it, the final loss of her slammed me. I sensed my siblings felt the same. Aged and shaken orphans, we processed behind the coffin and touched it our way to the pews of Holy Name, our childhood church.

Mom had said during the last month or so of her life that she had no idea what heaven was like, but that it had been "pretty darn good right here on earth," and that she was in no hurry to leave. I felt her spirit all around me that day, but where was she really now, I wondered?

We stood for the opening hymn, inhaled the incense used in funeral rites, drew comfort from relatives and friends who surrounded us. And then it was time for the homily.

Again, Father Murphy rose to the occasion.

"And so today we gather together to honor Arlene Bird," he said. "Arlene had a full and busy life as a farm wife and mother of eight children. But for those of us who know her, we can imagine her now in heaven. She is not sitting around, basking in the fact that she has made it. No. For Arlene's gift was connecting with people and remembering them. We can see her now, shaking hands with Saint Peter. He is trying to introduce her to some of the people there, but most of them..." and here Mom's priest pauses for effect... "she already knows."

Indeed, Father Murphy, indeed.

How beautiful (and funny!) that her spirit would be captured so succinctly by her priest. How lovely that her life would be honored in Holy Name, the baptismal church of her eight children, and the church of Dad's funeral.

At the end of Mom's life, it was just the right touch: the solemn familiarity of a Catholic funeral mass, plus light-hearted words from a priest who knew her well. There could be a no more fitting and final way to honor Mom: a soul forever intertwined with faith.

Self Esteem

Mom and Dad were not coddled as kids. Born in the 1920s, they grew up during the Depression and completely missed the self-esteem bandwagon. They were not given choices of breakfast cereal, enrolled in camps, or consulted on where they would like to go on vacation (or even go on vacation, for that matter.) They missed whole months of school to work on the farm (Mom in eighth grade) and traveled with neighboring farmers on "milk holidays" to dump out milk in protest of the low prices in the early 1930s (Dad). Being a kid was a serious business then. You helped out. You did as you were told. You were important to the livelihood of the farm; as soon as you were able, you contributed to the whole.

Coming from that background, they raised their own children along the same lines. They didn't concern themselves too much with our self-esteem, our self-confidence, or our self-worth. We were given jobs to do as soon as we were capable, and they saw nothing unusual in that. Just as we were expected to wake up and breathe each day, we were expected to work. A three-year-old could pick up toys, a five-year-old could give a bottle, a ten-year-old could cook a meal.

Did we mind? Yes and no. For to us, also, helping around the house and the farm was just what we did. We never languished in bed, stretching with delight at the prospect of a wide-open day, wondering how we might fill it.

"Time to get up!" Mom would yell upstairs no later than 7 o'clock on weekends and during the summer.

We'd hang up our pajamas, slip on t-shirts, cotton shorts, and canvas "tennis" shoes, scramble for the bathroom, and be downstairs at the dining room table in no less than 15 minutes.

And with that, our day began.

Confidence Building Jobs

<u>Taking care of the younger kids</u> -

I leaned over the bassinet and smelled the baby. No one else had ever mentioned it, but to me a newborn baby, a days old newborn, smelled exactly like a little piglet. This baby was chubby, his eyes were closed, and his name was Joe. It was the month of Mary and Fatima – October – and we were in the living room saying the rosary. I marveled at him. How was it possible that just a few days before he had been inside of mom?

I was six years old and Joe was to be my first real baby job. He loved his bottle and kicked his feet in the high chair when I sat down across from him with a bowl of hot oatmeal. He laughed when I pretended the spoon was an airplane landing in his mouth. "Oatmeal Joe" was a good baby and didn't squirm too much when I changed him. I carried him around on my hip wherever I went and mom used to say that's what made him bowlegged.

When I was busy helping mom with something else, Jane took over baby Joe duties.

Jane and I helped with the little ones in any way we could: diapering, feeding, bathing, and just in general, occupying the babies, pretty much all under Mom's supervision. But there came a time, when we were about nine and ten, when Mom and Dad thought Jane and I were responsible enough to babysit Mary and the boys. They left us ON OUR OWN, and went to play cards at the neighbors, just a mile down the road.

I remember feeling the immensity of the situation: I was in charge. I wasn't nervous; I felt the power of being the big boss and it felt GOOD. With Jane's help, I would do a perfect job.

I ran into my first challenge with Jeff, who dared to defy my authority. When it came time for the boys to go to bed, he simply said, "No."

I was shocked by his audacity; how dare he defy me? But repeating my instructions and repeating them louder and louder was ineffective: he just wasn't going to go to bed, period. Finally, in direct opposition to my authority, he shot me in the forehead with a rubber dart.

That was it. I was stunned by his rebelliousness and the dart had fueled a new kind of ferocious anger in me. I grabbed him around the neck in a headlock and dragged him up the stairs with him kicking the whole way. I threw him in his bed and that was that.

Or so I thought.

A bit later the boys called me up to their room on the pretense of a fight that couldn't be settled. I went storming up the stairs, all pistons firing, and burst through the partially opened door – only to have a large heavy hassock fall on my head. The boys collapsed in laughter; but no matter. They had won their little battle, but they knew they had pushed me to the limit and stayed in their beds after that, giving me at least the pretense of winning the war.

Doing the dishes and making our beds-

We ate all our meals together, so doing dishes was a three-times-a day affair that was actually quite streamlined. There were hardly ever leftovers to put away, and any scrapings from the pans or plates went right outside to the dog. One of the girls washed and one dried. The other swept the floor and wiped down the table, with Mom running interference to settle any questions about whose turn it was to do what. Without the convenience of a dishwasher, we were able to get along with a minimum of plates, glasses, and silverware.

Not making our beds would have been as inconceivable as if we had decided to walk on our hands for the day. We got up, put our pillows in place, pulled up our covers, and patted out the wrinkles. Perhaps this was done even before our trip to the bathroom. I'm not sure. But I do know it was done before breakfast.

Taking care of the chickens –

Every year just before Easter, we went to the hatchery in town and got our new baby chicks in big cardboard boxes. They peeped and pecked inside the box and if you accidentally turned the box on a slant, their tiny claws scraped on the cardboard as they slid to one side. Mom put the 200 of them in the chicken shed under a brooder light, which was a low box with open sides that was heated with light bulbs to keep the chicks warm. They needed to be fed and watered every day and that was the girls' job. We carried water in five-gallon metal buckets from the pump near the barn, holding one arm out to the side for balance so as not to slosh too much water on ourselves. We scooped chicken mash from a sack in the chicken shed with a coffee can and dumped it in a long low feeder. After a few days, the chicks got used to us and would peep and run toward the feeder when we came in.

In a very short time, the rooster chicks changed from tiny yellow balls to small white chicks with red combs and beady eyes. They roamed about the farm during the day and clustered in the chicken house at night, unaware that their freewheeling time pecking bugs in the farmyard would be short lived. Most of them only lived three or four months before we started to "process" them, which meant they ended up frozen in the deep chest freezer on the back porch. (We would butcher about 200 of them to stock up for the long winter ahead.)

We (either mom or one of the girls) caught them the night before they were to be butchered by snatching a leg with a long wire hook and stuffing them into a chicken crate, which held six to eight chickens. The next morning, Mom would place big vats of water on the stove, and while the pots heated to a boil, we'd go outside and use the same "chicken snatchers" to re-retrieve, one by one, the caught chickens from the crate. Grabbing the chicken by its legs, Mom would place it on the ground, then fold back its wings and kneel on them. She'd center its tiny neck over a board; a thin film of a lid would slide over the chicken's eye one last time and then with a bit of pressure and a quick slice of her knife, the deed would be over. She'd fling the head in one direction and the body in another, where it would flop and flip in the yard, somehow seeming alive without its head, until all its energy was spent, save for a weak last fluttering of wings in the dust. I was morbidly fascinated with the beheading of the chickens, on one hand horrified and on the other, honored, that I might be expected to kill chickens myself someday. Eventually, maybe when I was about twelve, that day came to pass, and despite my fears, I was able to saw/ push a knife through a rooster's neck and toss his body into the dusty yard.

After the chickens were all decapitated, Mom would fetch the boiling water from the kitchen and we'd take the carcasses by their feet, one by one and dip them into the water, swirling them to ensure that all the feathers were saturated, and thus loosened. We'd spin around in a circle with each sodden chicken body to fling off the excess water and then, when the birds had cooled just a little, we'd quickly go to work stripping the feathers, which had been released from their base by the boiling water and came off easily.

When we girls were young, we weren't expected to take part in the actual butchering, but we helped mom pack the pieces of chicken in waxy reused half-gallon milk containers. We watched her carefully, though, as she deftly sliced away the legs from the body, then hacked off the wings, next cut into the soft tissue under the breastbone, and finally pulled out the guts, still warm from the barely dead chicken.

"This is the heart...lungs...liver," she'd tell us as she cut away. "And this is the gizzard," she'd instruct us. "See, a chicken doesn't have a stomach like us. It has to peck up little stones that settle in the gizzard and grind the food inside." We wrinkled our noses at first, but then gradually got used to the sight and smell of the insides of a chicken. Good thing, as perhaps by the time we were twelve, we would be butchering chickens right beside her.

Cooking and baking:

With eight active, growing, and busy kids, food never soured, grew moldy, or was thrown away because no one liked it. Food was mostly eaten with abandon: chicken (of course, see above!), beef and pork, were served in a three-day rotation with potatoes and gravy. Food was simple (I tasted pasta for the first time in college), but plentiful. Meals were constantly being prepared and served and we girls helped from an early age: setting the table as soon as we could, then warming up vegetables, and by ten or so, making an entire meal, to include cooking the meat. I know because I have a very vivid memory of burning my arm with hot grease from frying chicken. The others were out in the field, walking beans, and I had been entrusted to make the entire noon "dinner," which in the summer was our main meal.

The potatoes were peeled and boiling, the table was set, and some kind of vegetable was stewing on the stove. I was frying the chicken in hot lard. There was a startling pop in the pan, the skin separated from the meat, and drops of hot grease splattered on my arm. I didn't know enough to put my arm under cold water right away and red ovals formed up and down my arm, turning into blisters by the afternoon. A few days later, Mom treated us to an afternoon at the Marcus town pool. By then, the

47

burns were more ugly than painful, but I wasn't so self-conscious about the "bubbles" running up and down my arm that I would chose to stay home.

"Ee-oh, what happened to your arm?" I remember one of the town girls saying at the pool, as she grimaced at my oozing blisters.

I shrugged, not wanting to explain, and quickly escaped with a dive into the cool blue water.

****

To satisfy eight hungry kids, we girls baked almost every day: oatmeal cookies, chocolate chip cookies, chocolate drop cookies, honey hermits, raisin sugar cookies, Mazola oil brownies and never-fail chocolate cake, to name a few. There was a cookie jar on the kitchen counter, but it typically held just a few cookies at the bottom, as we usually ate almost a whole batch of anything at a sitting. A favorite was honey- glazed donuts, which took Jane and I the whole morning to make. If it was a donut day, we would make the bread-like dough by nine o'clock and let it rise for an hour. At ten o'clock, (when it should have doubled in size), we removed the dough from the bowl, punched it down, rolled it out, cut out the donut shapes, placed them on pans to rise a second time, and waited another hour. Around eleven, when the donuts had doubled in size again, we dropped them one by one in hot oil, and carefully flipped them over with long handled tongs (remember the chicken burn!), letting each side turn a golden brown. After the donuts had cooled and drained on racks, we dipped them into a thin sugary glaze and sampled one or two, just to make sure they were fit to eat.

No matter that our noon meal was always a hearty combination of meat, potatoes, vegetables, and gravy; no matter that we all had to have substantial servings; and no matter that we had to clean our plates: everyone had room for donuts. At the end of the meal, the entire batch was placed in the middle of the table and we grabbed and gobbled from that white enamel container until there wasn't a single donut left.

Not one.

That's right. Not one single, cholesterol-laden, sugar-filled, carbohydrate-packed donut.

As if we cared, coyote pups that we were. We knew nothing of the horrible health hazards in each of those airy sweet things. We cared not a whit that for each donut we ate, we might lose as much as a day of life. Heck, we did not know that we might die a whole week earlier if we could eat seven donuts at one sitting!

Who cared? We ate with abandon and pure, untainted gluttony. Donuts were the present and the present was good.

Working in the garden

When I was very little and it was nearly impossible for mom to get off the farm, the "grocery man" from Germantown came by the farm once a week. He'd knock on the screen door on Tuesdays, pencil behind his ear, and then take mom's carefully constructed grocery list to his truck. I'd watch him from the gate of the "little yard" (the fenced in area near the house) as he filled the list, pulling cereal, flour, sugar, and dry goods from the shelves inside the multiple doors of his truck. I could hardly wait for him to finish, for I knew he would leave a heaping box of groceries on the chair just inside the back-porch door and inside that box – somewhere – would be one pack of spearmint Juicy Fruit gum – free!

Even though the grocery man came to our house for a few years, Mom always had a vegetable garden, which grew exponentially as the family expanded. She was the absolute matriarch of the garden: selecting what to plant, deciding where to put each vegetable, and directing we kids, her often reluctant maintenance squad, in taking care of it.

In the spring, we learned to cut up seed potatoes, making sure each piece had an "eye," then dug 3-4-inch holes to plant them each about a foot apart. We learned that if the Iowa weather permitted, potatoes were best planted around St. Joseph's day, March 19th. We learned to sprinkle the tiny black lettuce and radish seeds in shallow troughs in early May so that they could be harvested before the dog days of summer turned them bitter. We learned how to prune tomato plants, pinching off the spindly sucker shoots that sapped the sturdier branches and robbed the fruit of nutrients. And we learned that unless you staked the plants, they would break under the burden of their own mother lode and rot on the ground. We learned approximately how long it took each kind of plant to bear fruit and how to harvest everything: peas, green beans, beets, potatoes, radishes, cabbage, lettuce, tomatoes, squash, pumpkins, cantaloupes, watermelons, and cucumbers. But when I think of the garden, most of all, I remember hoeing.

Planting the garden was a hopeful beginning, the exciting launch of a vision of lush even rows, laden with vegetables. Hoeing was repetitive and backbreaking work. With a garden close to a half-acre in size, hoeing was never really "finished," even for the week. We were assigned patches for an afternoon, usually with a partner: the green beans and the potatoes, the tomatoes, the lettuce and radishes, or worst of all- the melon and pumpkin patch.

Even after sharpening our hoes – sparks flying off the stone fly wheel in the tool shed– the hoe seemed to dull itself on the way to the vast and infinite melon patch. When we needed rain, we broke through the crusty earth with fierce chopping – the turned over earth just a shade darker for all our efforts. When the soil was wet, it stuck to the blade of the hoe in a heavy clump that flew off only when it reached critical mass – a seeming thousand pounds.

In the heat of July, I couldn't remember the perfectly ripe pink-splitting pop as a knife sunk into the rind of a September melon, the sugary warm sweetness of gorging ourselves on watermelon after school, standing in the yard and tossing our rinds over the fence to the chickens. I didn't think of the pumpkin pies mom made every week in the fall, full bodied with pulp, heaping with both calories and whipped cream.

No, I thought only of the size of the darn patch, the ache in my back, and the blister on the inside of my right thumb. That and the fact that once Jane and I finished for the day, it'd be Tom and Jeff's turn next week, as we'd temporarily served our time.

Which is why, after years of hoeing in the garden, a seemingly innocent high school high school prank took on such epic proportions for me. Twice in the fall of my junior year, classmates of mine came at night, snuck in our garden, and smashed pumpkins and melons to their ignorant delight. We pressed our faces to the window screens, absorbing their violations, as peals of laughter drifted across the dark, impassive yard. (See "Smashing Pumpkins.")

Walking Beans

Today Midwestern farmers use massive amounts of pesticides and herbicides, resulting in acres and acres of weed-free crops. But that wasn't the case when we were growing up. There was "2-4-D" and little else. The way to achieve those rolling, clean-as-a-whistle fields of soybeans - unbroken by unsightly pockets of button weeds, cockleburs, thistles, milk weeds, and corn - was simple: use your kids!

"Walking beans" probably only took about 3 weeks of our summer, but to me, it seemed that we did it every day, all day for 3 months. For it was boring, tedious, and hot work that seared itself into memory. Basically, it went like this: walk down length of the row to nearest road (usually about a half mile) while pulling out every weed on the way, turn around, and repeat on way back. Begin in the morning, work until 11:45, eat dinner, return to field. Finish about 4:00. Look forward to reward of swimming in

Paullina Lake, and perhaps even a root beer float after that.

The saving grace of walking beans was that we did it as a group; it was not as if one or two of us or even just the boys were singled out for this onerous job. EVERYBODY, including mom and dad, went to the field, unless we were too young (probably five and under) or cooking dinner (see above). If it was muddy and the soil caked on our old sneakers in heavy clumps, it happened to us all. If the beans were bushy and covered the space between the rows, the wet leaves and stems slashed at all of our ankles as we walked. If the temperature soared into the 90s, no one got a pass because they couldn't take the heat. And with nine people working, we could do over a hundred rows in a round and sometimes finish a field in a morning. We could easily stop at any moment and see just how much we had accomplished, surveying the weed-free soybean fields to our left and behind, the secret seed of self-esteem sprouting inside.

Acknowledging Accomplishments

Mom and Dad were anything but lavish in their praise of our hard work and achievements. For a long time, even as an adult, I chafed at the memory of a couple of mom's painful remarks. A favorite of hers, usually uttered when she was trying to show me how to do something, was the classic: "For someone as smart as you, how can you be so stupid?" Part of the answer might have been that the person who was teaching me (Mom) was both innately smarter than me and caught on to things much more quickly than I did, for I was a plodding, dogged learner. There were certainly other hurtful remarks, but one I remember best happened when I was a teenager, dashing out the door to be picked up for a date. I had angsted over my clothes for almost an hour, trying and re-trying on my few outfits, and then finally decided that I looked the best in a particular one.

I raced down the steps to the waiting car, not wanting to subject my date to mom's interrogation. (Strangely, mom and dad didn't demand that we introduce our dates to them.) Just before I reached the car, the screen door opened and mom gave a parting shot.

"You look like hell!" she yelled.

I slammed the car door, settled into my seat, and flashed my date a practiced smile.

"Hey," he said, putting the car into gear, "what did your mom just say?"

"Nothing," I said, "nothing big. Let's just go."

****

Looking back from the advantage of being a parent myself, I can see that there were unspoken perks of doing work as a child. The work itself produced its own rewards. Without someone telling us over and over that we were responsible and capable – we became responsible and capable. It just happened. Without someone defining the characteristics of a good leader, we developed those characteristics from managing small projects and, in some cases, managing our younger siblings. As adults, we do not have to have our own way; we understand that others' opinions have value, too. And for the most part, as adults, we get along with others because we had to as kids. No one actually taught us about cooperation and group processes; we lived that mentality from birth on.

Digging deeper, I admit there were actually a number of examples of mom and dad's acknowledgements of our accomplishments. Each quarter, when report cards were issued, we were treated to supper at Lange's Café, a local diner. Not one of us was singled out for exceptional grades; we were all rewarded with a hamburger, French fries, and a malted milk shake. Our treat was that we got to pick the flavor: did we want strawberry, chocolate, or vanilla? Mom and Dad also went to every parent teacher conference, despite the fact that most of us didn't need them to, signaling how important our education was.

Another incident comes to mind: Mom taking time on a spring Sunday to attend a diocesan awards ceremony when I received a poetry award in 8th grade. She drove all the way to Carroll, Iowa to see me in a 30 second flash as I crossed the stage, received a medal from the bishop, and shook his hand. This moment is etched in my memory as SOMETHING IMPORTANT; not for the praise mom lavished on me (she didn't), but because her presence meant the accomplishment was significant.

Yet as we made our way through school and life, Mom was keeping track of our achievements. Despite her chockfull-of-activity life, she somehow managed to clip local newspaper articles of our accomplishments, save programs of our graduations, and organize significant photos for each of us, individually. She compiled all these together in a scrapbook, which we each received at graduation - without effusive praise - every memento secured with black corner tags and carefully labeled as to year and event.

I played high school basketball, as did most of us, and I clearly remember waiting for the buzzer to start the game and seeing Mom and Dad - with his navy-blue stocking cap pulled low over his forehead – walk into the gym. Why that stocking cap bothered me, I can't say; only that in my self-absorbed teenage world, it was a source of embarrassment. It was also a symbol of their steadfast support in the dead of those Iowa winters - even if the temperature were to dip below zero and even if Dad had to wear an old dull stocking cap to keep warm – they were going to be present at those games. To their credit, they never screamed at us from the sidelines (not at me, anyway); they never rehashed my missed free throws or layup opportunities; they never suggested that I hustle a little more or be aggressive. They never criticized our coach or any of the other players.

In fact, when I became a junior and Jane took my place on the starting lineup, they didn't pity me or extol Jane. They said nothing until I came to them in the middle of the night, heartbroken and unable to sleep. I was humiliated at sitting the bench, devastated that I had been demoted and that my younger sister had taken my place.

"It's not that important," Dad murmured sleepily, when I woke them up. "In five years, none of this will matter."

"Try to say the rosary," Mom would say, sounding much more compassionate in the dark than in the harsh light of day.

Although their responses didn't make the pain go away, they were correct in not trying to "fix" me. They didn't advise me to practice more free throws or run in my free time to increase my speed. They didn't tell me to talk to the coach, nor talk to him themselves. They never said they felt sorry for me. They never told me that I was a great basketball player just the way I was (we all knew better!), nor suggested that this set back was just temporary and I would someday be great. In fact, they suggested nothing to do with basketball itself.

Yet somehow through their lack of specific direction, I knew. From their spoken middle-of-the-night responses, I knew that my athletic performance really wasn't that important to them, only as much as I let it affect me. I knew that mostly they wanted me to feel better about myself and that giving me specific basketball suggestions to "help" me perform would have only put more pressure on me.

And from the silence in between those responses, I knew that love hung heavy in the air of that bedroom; I could sense that love as they weighed their responses and listened to me in the middle of the night. I was important to them as their daughter, not a great basketball player. And they would still come to the games no matter how I played, their presence honoring my efforts.

Maybe mom and dad could have been more demonstrative, maybe they could have complimented us more, maybe they could have spent some time with us

57

individually, praising our unique abilities and accomplishments, but the fact is -

for the most part, they didn't. They had not grown up in praise-heaped environments themselves.

Perhaps this is why – with this paucity of praise received himself – that dad found it so difficult, yet necessary, to sit down on my bed as I packed for college. So unusual was his presence in my room that I stopped what I was doing.

"Well, Kathy," he said, hesitating in unfamiliar territory, "I just want to say that you are a really good girl. We are proud of you."

"Oh," I said, having no ready words of gratitude, as this was unfamiliar territory for me, too. "Oh."

"I just wanted to tell you," he said.

Other daughters and fathers might have hugged each other right then and let their love gush back and forth body-to-body, but this was not to be with us. At that moment, hugging dad would have been as likely as if I had broken into an Irish jig and danced into the hall: hugging was not something we were we were familiar with or practiced at all.

"Okay," I said my arms stiffly at my side.

And with that, Dad left the room as quietly as he had entered it.

I sat on the bed for a long, long time. Without knowing why, I began to cry. Was it because I had waited such a long time for my efforts at everything - school, being a good daughter, a good sister- to be recognized? Was it because I finally felt recognized for just being me, a unique individual? Was it because I sensed how difficult it was for Dad to praise me, even though I knew he spoke from his heart?

Perhaps it was for a bit of all these reasons and more that tears came unbidden then, as I packed to leave the security of everything I knew. Perhaps that is why, nearly fifty years later, tears fall again even as I write these words.

The Gopher Games

Easter 1960
Left to right: Tom, Kathy holding Joe, Mary, Jane, and Jeff

The Gopher Games

Long before *The Hunger Games* riveted millions to
the screen, we Bird cousins of Iowa had our very own
unique sport—one with just the right touch of violence
and competition to make it a much loved and sacred
Easter tradition. The Gopher Hunt was an ingenious
activity devised by Dad with a three-fold purpose. It got
the cousins outside and out of Mom's hair when we
hosted all the Birds for Easter. It was a physical activity
that involved skill and speed and tired us out. And – by
clubbing the drowning and gasping gophers to death – we
were decimating the farm's destructive rodent population
to boot.

It was a glorious, if unusual, way to celebrate
Easter.

Sure, we all attended Easter Mass in the morning.
We girls wore new hats secured to our heads with white
snappy elastic bands and shivered in our pastel dresses.
The boys sported hand-me-down suits and slim clip-on
ties. In church, we dutifully prayed for each other, our
parents and grandparents, the poor children throughout
the world, and an extra piece of bacon at breakfast. We
squinted into the cold sun for the obligatory Easter photo,
standing next to the wall of the house, the side of our
station wagon, or a fence that needed painting—anything
that could be a backdrop for a gang of kids.

Meanwhile, Mom continued her own personal
prayer, a novena of sorts that she had started at least nine
days before the holiday. Since we always hosted Easter,
meaning we had twenty plus cousins and eight or so aunts

and uncles on the farm for the day, and there was no guarantee of the Iowa weather in March or April, Mom's novena went like this:

"Jesus Christ, don't let it rain."

"Oh God, I can't have all those kids in my house."

"Christ, I hope the mud dries up before Easter."

Over and over during the week or so before Easter, she repeated these petitions and as Sunday drew closer, she increased her weather vigilance. She pored over the forecast in the Sioux City Journal, she listened to KCHE while she ironed, and she kept a trained eye on the barometer.

But we Bird cousins were oblivious. We didn't care if it rained or not; we didn't even care if it snowed a little. Nothing short of a tornado could stop us: Easter was gopher-hunting time and we couldn't wait!

While mom took her prayers to a fever pitch on Holy Saturday, dad worked on his assignment of filling a large tank in the bed of our Chevy pickup with ice-cold well water. He attached a long hose to the tank and as soon as the bulk of the cousins arrived on Easter, he was at the ready to follow Mom's orders and institute phase two of the gopher games:

"Get those damn kids outside as soon as you can!"

Out of Easter finery for hours and wearing farm play clothes, the cousins all traipsed into the grove in search of the perfect gopher club. This took a good while—though never as long as dad had envisioned—because the club could neither be too big nor too small for its bearer. Of course, a thick tree limb would be quite effective against a defenseless little gopher, but could you actually heft it over your head to do the job? On the other hand, the more seasoned gopher hunters had all experienced the excruciating agony of having a small limb snap in two on the first gopher, rendering the hunter useless for the rest of the day.

You just had to have the right club.

Once the twenty or so of us were armed, the little ones squeezed into the cab of the truck with dad. The older ones stood on the running board and held on through the open windows or sat upon the tank, and a few of the more daring sat on the hood. Dad drove slowly out the yard—through dust or mud, depending on the year—and into the unplanted fields. We gripped our clubs and kept our eyes peeled for the telltale signs of a gopher home sweet home—a sad and sorry little hole in the ground.

"Is that one, Uncle Bill?" one of the cousins would yell and dad would slow the truck from a crawl to something almost like reverse.

"Well, let's try it and see," he'd say and we'd whoop with delight. Unwrapping the hose, he'd stick the end in the unsuspecting rodent foyer and then turn on the spigot. If we were lucky, within minutes a slicked back gopher head would appear, gasping for air.

"There it is!" we'd yell, wired with adrenaline, and smash our clubs with abandon. Mud would spatter and the poor gopher would sometimes retreat in fear. But alas, a gopher can only hold its breath so long, and it would always pop up again to its grisly demise.

"Get him!" we'd yell if the gopher somehow managed to escape both his hole and our frenzied clubbing. We'd give chase and almost always one of the more athletic cousins would claim the kill.

We never thought about animal cruelty; we never thought of the little gopher's pain and suffering. We never thought that perhaps a gopher had a right to his own gopher life and a little bit of gopher happiness. We might have been satisfied that on some level we were helping the farm by getting rid of varmints, and we were proud when it was our very own club that had scored a hit. But mostly, we were just having fun.

AND celebrating Easter in our own quirky Bird cousin way.

Easter 1964
Back row: Kathy, Jeff, Tom, Jane
Front row: Mary, Mike, Joe, Pat

Smashing Pumpkins

One night in September of my junior year, Mom and Dad went to an open house at the school. Jane, Mary, and I were cleaning up after supper; Tom and Jeff were doing homework at the dining room table, and the "little boys" (Joe, Mike, and Pat – 7,8, and 9 years old) were wrestling, their bodies a mass of arms and legs, rolling around the living room floor.

"If you're going to fight, get outside!" I ordered them, ever the big sister in charge. Dusk had just fallen on the farm and a fat full moon sat on the horizon. The air was warm, balmy almost, and the lawn was bathed in a gray white sheen – a perfect evening for them to be out of the house.

"Go! Go!" I shooed them with my dishtowel. "Get out. Now."

They grumbled, but obeyed, the screen door banging behind them.

But within minutes, Joe shot back into the house again.

"You gotta come out! You gotta come outside!" he said. "It's robbers or murderers or something! Something's going on out there!"

I stopped drying the cast iron skillet in my hand. "Slow down," I said. "What are you talking about?"

"There's an old truck that keeps going by our place!"

"So?" I said and set the skillet on the stove.

"Well, it's been by like five times!"

"So?" Jane echoed.

"So, it slows way down – like it's going to stop – every time it goes by our lane! It must be murderers or something! C'mon!" Joe tugged on my shirt. "C'mon!" he said again.

"It's not murderers," I said. "Trust me."

"Well, it's got to be bad guys or something! You gotta come out!"

"All right. All right," I said. I could feel my heart pick up. I was in charge. Was something really wrong?

"You coming, too?" I said to Jane and Mary. It wasn't backups I was thinking of just then, but two more witnesses to see how goofy my little brothers were.

They nodded and we followed Joe outside, ducking under the clothesline, and then pausing near the swing set as he motioned us to stop.

"Hear that?" he said.

We cocked our heads and there it was: a backfiring vehicle coming from the west, maybe a half mile away. He waved us forward, got down on all fours, and started Army crawling toward the road.

"Get down!" he said. "We can't let them see us!"

Jane, Mary, and I looked at each other, shrugged, and got down on our bellies. We pulled ahead like soldiers squirming under barbwire, until we reached Mike and Pat, who were scrunched down in the moonlit grass, waiting for us near the fence by the road.

"Now listen!" Joe hissed.

"That's it! Hear it?" Mike said.

"Do you think it's bad guys?" Pat whispered.

"Nah." I raised my head from the grass to reassure him. "What would bad guys be doing here?" Bad guys were in places like New York City and Los Angeles and robbed rich people of diamonds and money. Bad guys wouldn't come to a farm in Iowa.

"It's just somebody coming home from town," I said.

The vehicle – I could tell it was a pickup by now – bore down on us and sure enough, downshifted when it got close. It passed directly in front of us – an older farm truck I didn't recognize- and then the driver shut off the engine. The truck rolled to a stop not more than 25 yards away, gravel crunching beneath its wheels in the still, silver night.

I could hear my pulse in my ears. What the heck was going on?

We flattened ourselves even lower to the ground. The pickup doors opened. Through the tufts of grass at the bottom of the wire fence, we saw figures drop from the truck into the ditch.

"People are getting out of the truck!" Joe said. "What's going to happen? What are we going to do?"

"What we're going to do is stay right here for now and be very quiet!" I whispered, trying to sound as brave as possible. Unlike school, where I struggled to manage just about any social situation, I was supposed to be in my element here. I was in charge. But what if these guys – whoever they were - tried to hurt the kids or me? What if they came after us?

"I'm scared!" Mary whined.

"They're going in the field!" Jane said. "Did you see that?"

"What are we going to do?" Joe said again.

"Sh-h-h! Everybody shush!" I said. "Stay low. Stay very low. When I think it's safe, we'll crawl back to the house."

Gone from sight, we could hear the intruders crash into the field, crunching and breaking soybean stalks. Hurried insistent voices cut the still night – male voices – but the words were indistinguishable as of yet. What were they doing? If they were going to rob the house, maybe they were going to approach it in a roundabout way? Maybe they were going to storm the front door? How would we warn Tom and Jeff, who were inside, oblivious to everything going on?

And then the voices took on a different tone. No longer urgent or intense, they rose and fell about us, floating to our hideout in the grass. We strained to make out the words. The rustling in the soybean field stopped and I thought I heard something else, something that didn't make sense to me, lying timid and fearful on the lawn.

"Are they laughing?" Jane whispered.

"I don't get it. Why would they laugh?" Mike said.

"It sounds like they're in the garden now," Mary said.

And then, clearly on the night air: "Old man Bird...pumpkin patch..."

More laughter.

"Hey shut up! They'll hear us!"

"This is wild, man!"

"Quiet, you moron!"

A sickening splat followed. Then one giddy almost high-pitched peal of laughter. More splats. And then a chorus of gleeful howling; rowdies reveling in the otherwise quiet night.

"I think they're smashing our pumpkins," Mary said. "Why would they be doing that?"

I knew then that we weren't in danger. Our house wouldn't be robbed or torched. We wouldn't be murdered. Or kidnapped. Or held hostage. I knew then that we wouldn't even be physically harmed in any way.

For the voices in the field were ones I now recognized. Football players from my very own high school, guys who sat beside me in history class, or had the same study hall, or might have been on my team in gym. I should have been angry that they dared to come on our land without permission. I should have been angry that they were brazen enough to wreck our garden. I should have been angry that they had scared my brothers. And maybe just a little bit I was.

But more than that, I felt something else, something I couldn't quite identify. They could have come to any farm, but they had picked ours. Was it me? Was it somehow targeted toward me? Wasn't it enough that I felt like a nobody in school, a gawky girl who said little in class? Wasn't it enough that one question: "Hey, Bird, isn't it about time you shaved your legs?" had intimidated me for a whole semester?

Did they have to come to our farm, too?

****

69

When Mom and Dad came home that night, we all clamored to tell them what had happened.

"We were so scared," one of the little boys said.

"Yeah, they came in an old truck," said another. "And it kept slowing down by our place!"

"They smashed our pumpkins!"

"What are we gonna do?"

Dad listened carefully and rubbed his chin.

They'll be back, was all he said.

****

The next day, we went out with Dad to survey the damage. The garden was trampled. Orange pumpkin flesh was everywhere. We had helped Mom plant the pumpkins in late spring, tucking three seeds in each mound placed five feet apart. We kids had taken turns hoeing the patch throughout the summer, moving the long tendrils out of the way to scrape away weeds, longing for August when finally, the vines fully covered the dirt. It took a whole summer – all ninety days of it – to grow a pumpkin and finally – just now - they were ripe for Mom's signature pies.

I could see that Dad was thinking about what to do. He climbed into the tree house at the end of the lane and looked down at the patch. I knew from there he could get a good view of things.

That night he told us that he was still figuring it out. He had thought about taking his shotgun in the tree house and firing it off in the air when the boys came back. Not to hurt them, he said, but just to scare them a little. But then he thought, what good would that do, just to scare them? He really wanted to know who they were and why they would do such a thing. He wanted to hear them say that they were sorry. No, he decided, frightening them would not be enough. And besides, there was the small chance that even with firing a gun into the air, someone could get hurt.

I'll have to think about it more, he said.

****

When I slid into my assigned seat in history class after the weekend across the aisle from Jimmy (name changed), one of the pumpkin smashers, I kept my eyes down and pulled out my homework.

"Hey, man, that was so cool the other night!" Jimmy said to one of his buddies, who sat in front of me.

"Yeah, what are we doing tonight?"

I opened my history book and scanned the title of the next chapter: "The United States Is Forced into World War II," it said. "Prior to 1941, the U.S. had maintained a policy of isolationism, but events in the world deemed that this could not continue. On December 7, 1941, the Navy in Pearl Harbor was stunned to..." My mind raced over the page, taking comfort in pronouncing the words in my head, yet not really comprehending any of them.

"Pick you up about 7," Jimmy said to his friend. "This time we'll go south of town, all right?"

"Sure thing," his friend answered.

Thankfully, the teacher interrupted their exchange. "Students! Students! Settle down now," he said. "Please pass your assignments forward."

I turned to get the papers from the girl behind me and my own paper slid off the desk, drifted to the floor, and landed right by Jimmy's foot.

"Hey, pumpkin head," he said lazily bending down to pick it up. "Did you drop this?"

****

Over the next week, Dad immersed himself in the relentless demands of the harvest, the combine and cornpicker clacking almost continuously in order to take advantage of the weather. Mom tackled her work with constant, almost superhuman vigor: washing ten loads of laundry twice a week, cooking hearty suppers of meat and vegetables from the farm, mending, ironing, cleaning, and overseeing the little boys' homework. They said nothing of the intruders who had vandalized the garden and neither did we. But all the while we were listening, listening for the sounds of an old truck in the night.

Finally, on a Friday night, about ten days later, Joe heard the unmistakable sound of a misfiring engine rumbling down the county road toward the house.

"It's them!" he told Dad.

Dad raced out of the house – what was he going to do? - and Jeff followed him.

The rest of us scrambled upstairs and opened the windows of the farmhouse. We crouched so only our heads cleared the sills, peered into the darkness and listened.

The pickup came by our house another time, and as before, stopped when it passed the lane. We heard truck doors open and slam, heard gravel crunch underfoot. Again, voices drifted to us, but this time to the safety of our bedrooms.

"Hey, man, this is wild.... hey, watch the fence...whadaya doin', man?"

By now it was October, and the moon had cycled to just a sliver in the sky. It was impossible to see what was happening in the garden. But we knew it was the same truck, the same boys, doing the same thing – smashing and stealing our pumpkins.

I felt my face get hot and I clenched my fists. Not only were these guys wrecking the garden – ruining a summer's worth of work, but they were sure to embarrass me again in school tomorrow. Wasn't there something that could be done?

And then: the sound of a car starting up, an engine revving, gravel spitting as our long green station wagon shot down the lane and out to the road. A car door opened and slammed shut. Muffled voices. Scrambling and rustling in the soybeans between the garden and the road.

"Get your hands off me!" one of the guys yelled.

"Who's in there with you? Who's in my field?" Dad yelled back.

Our eyes widened. Dad was out there and it sounded like he had somebody pinned to the ground. We didn't know it, but Jeff had hopped in the car with Dad and was trying to see what was going on from the safety of the front seat. He was scared for Dad with those big high school boys.

"C'mon, let me go!" the guy's voice was higher now, pleading.

"I'll let you go...when you tell me... who's in the field!" Dad said. He was panting now and I could imagine him shaking the guy a little bit, side to side.

"Come out! Come out you guys, right now!" the guy said, and I thought maybe he was going to cry.

More crackling in the soybeans.

"Run!"

"Let's...get...out...of...here!"

And then, "Where's my shoe?" someone whined. "My shoe fell off! I can't find my damn shoe!"

The voices weren't strong and cocky anymore. They were scared and broken up and out of breath, as if they were running away.

"What's going on?" Mary wondered aloud.

"Old man Bird's out here!" somebody yelled from the field. "Go! Go! Get out!"

"Oh my gosh, what's Dad doing?" I said. By now, I recognized at least one of the other voices and I was sure they were the same guys from the high school football team. Was Dad trying to strong-arm a big high school football player by himself?

"Is Dad going to be okay?" Mike wondered.

"Sounds like he's chasing them now!" said Jane.

"Sh-h! I can't hear!" somebody said.

Then there was swearing coming from the road.

"He took the keys! Shit, he took the God damned keys!"

"Dad took the keys! Dad took the keys to the truck!" Pat said. "And now they can't get away!"

"What's going to happen now?" asked Mike.

I was wondering the same thing. For a while we heard nothing more from the garden and then the screen door opened downstairs. There was mumbling in the porch. We moved to the top of the stairs and crouched there, straining to hear what was going on. After a bit, we could make out what Dad was saying.

"Why don't you boys just come into the dining room and tell me why you were in my garden?" he said.

"We didn't mean anything by it!" one of the boys said with an edge to his voice. I couldn't believe he would talk to Dad like that. I know I wouldn't.

"I said I want you to come into my dining room and tell me what you were doing in my garden," Dad repeated in a firm voice.

We could hear chairs scraping as the boys sat down at the table.

"Now," Dad said again, "would anyone like to tell me what you were doing in my garden?"

"C'mon," one of them said. "You know what we were doing in there."

"I'd like to hear it from you," Dad said, now with an edge to HIS voice.

Upstairs, we held our breath for what seemed like a long time.

Finally, one of the guys said they were just having a little bit of fun.

"You might have thought you were having fun," said Dad, "BUT WHAT WERE YOU DOING IN MY GARDEN?"

More silence.

Then at last Jimmy spoke up.

"We were smashing pumpkins," he said.

"Finally, an honest answer," Dad said. "Seems like a silly way to have fun. Is there any reason you'd do something like that for fun?"

I couldn't see Dad, but I could imagine him now, rubbing his chin again, just waiting.

No one said anything. It was quiet for a long time.

"They can't think of an answer!" said Pat.

Finally, Dad said, "Well, I guess maybe your parents would know why you'd trespass on other people's property and destroy things. I guess maybe I'll have to talk to each of them and ask them why their sons would do something like that."

More silence.

"All right. If you can't think of anything to say, I'm going to let you go tonight. But you might want to tell your parents what you've done. Let them know before they hear from me this weekend. Here are your keys," he said.

We could hear chairs scraping again as the pumpkin smashers got up, the screen door squeaked open and closed a few times, and then at last, there was a pop as the engine of the old truck started up and rumbled away.

We raced downstairs. "Hey dad, that was pretty cool that you took their keys!" "That one guy sounded like he was going to cry in the field! Who was that?" "Did somebody really lose his shoe in the garden?"

"Are you really going to talk to their parents?"

"Whoa. Whoa. Whoa," Dad motioned for us to quiet down.

"I just want to know what we'll do the next time they come?" Mary asked.

Everyone stopped talking and looked at Dad.

"You don't have to worry," he said. "You won't ever see them here again."

****

I listened for the sound of an old truck the rest of that fall, half expecting it to barrel down our road on any of those crisp October nights. I waited with my heart beating quietly, yet ever ready to pound, should the pumpkin smashers – my schoolmates – dare to return.

But Dad was right; they never did. Perhaps it was because he had scared them just a little, wrestling with them in the field. Perhaps it was because he did speak to their parents, even though he was unimpressed with their responses. Boys will be boys, they said, and I'm sure they are sorry. Perhaps it was because the season died and a cold hard frost chilled their antics. No matter; they did not come back.

The first snow fell early that year and with that, I felt relief.

But Can It Make a Hamburger?

My dad sits on a metal folding chair in the driveway of the three-bedroom ranch home to which he and mom retired when they left the farm. It's a hot July evening in Iowa and friends and family have gathered in honor of my parents 50th wedding anniversary, even though Mom and Dad were married on a frigid January day. After all, my parents are practical people and who would want to travel to Iowa for a celebration in January? Getting married in the dead of winter all those years ago was perhaps the first and last whimsical decision made by the two of them, but fortunately, their wedding day was snowless and all their guests arrived safely. They were lucky once, Mom says, and there is no sense in tempting fate fifty years later. Having their 50th anniversary party in July is a practical solution; a good alternative to having a party in January in northwest Iowa.

The red cooler in the garage holds Bud Lite for the adults; the blue—Hy-Vee pop for the grandkids. There are small bowls of peanuts on the folding tables to munch on and that's all. No need for avocado dip or salsa or sushi rolls for this post reception gathering; the guests have had their fill of ham sandwiches, mints, cake, and coffee in the church basement. Over two hundred people have made their way through the receiving line that afternoon, and all, except for a few out of town relatives, were summoned through an open invitation posted in the hometown *Marcus News*.

"You are invited to a 50th wedding anniversary for Arlene and Bill Bird from 2 to 5 p.m. in the Holy Name Church basement," the invitation read. "No presents please. Your presence is enough." It would be silly to send invitations and request RSVPs, reasoned my parents. This way, everyone—including my high school basketball coach, the Chevy dealer who sold my parents their last three cars, the local insurance agent who played keyboard at my wedding along with his wife on drums, the manager of the co-op elevator, the veterinarian who once reinserted our cow's prolapsed uterus, the grocer of our town's only food store—all are welcome to come to the anniversary party and they do. No one is slighted and no one is obligated. It all makes perfect sense.

Now that the official reception is over, my dad has shed his mandatory tie and his standard blue shirt is open at the neck. He's rubbing his chin, and though Parkinson's tempers his face, I can tell he's listening intently to my uncle Mick, who is sitting beside him on the driveway.

"Jeff's working on this tunnel that goes underground by Dallas," my uncle says, referring to his oldest son, my first cousin. He pushes his glasses up on his nose with his middle finger, crosses his leg, puts a hand on his hip, and leans in toward dad.

"It's a government project," he adds and looks around before he continues.

"A tunnel for cars?" my dad asks, ever the polite listener.

"No, it's not for cars, Bill," my uncle says. He leans back in his chair and frowns. It seems he is exasperated by dad's question.

"Is it for subways or something like that?" my dad asks.

"No, it's nothing like that," my uncle says and now he's clearly frustrated. "It's this big giant tunnel," he says and spreads his arms wide. "It's called a Supercollider."

"Actually, it's kind of secret," he says a bit too loudly for any secret, government or otherwise. He looks over his shoulder again. "Christ, it's about fifty miles around," he says. "All underground."

"What is it for, Mick?" my dad says. He's perplexed now and I am, too.

"It takes atoms and gets them going real fast all the hell around and smashes them," Mick says.

My dad waits – maybe there is more of an explanation. I'm wondering, too.

"And what do they do in the tunnel?" my dad finally asks.

"What?"

"The atoms," my dad says and leans towards Mick. He's really trying to understand.

"Christ, Bill, they make things in the supercollider!" my uncle says, and throws up his hands, as if to say we should all know the business of atoms.

"Like what?" dad asks. I know he's trying to visualize something concrete, something to touch, or see, or smell or taste—something knowable through the senses. Me, too.

"Anything!" my uncle says. "It can make anything."

Dad rubs his chin again, the familiar gesture that means he is processing what's just been said. He shrugs

80

and gets down to the nitty gritty of practicality, of needs, of all things tangible and useful.

"Well," he says, with a perfectly straight face, "can it make a hamburger?"

If Mick had been exasperated with the conversation before this point, by now he was beyond flummoxed.

"No," he sputters, "for God's sake, Bill, you can't make HAMBURGERS in the Supercollider!"

I'm assuming that soon after we changed the conversation to Jackie, Mick's next-in-line daughter, for I don't remember ever settling on what exactly the Supercollider did.

Interestingly enough, the Supercollider didn't ever get a chance to make anything. It was indeed a giant circular tunnel under the ground and south of Dallas that would have had a circumference of about 54 miles. The whole community of Waxahachie, Texas banked on the $4 billion plus project and the revenue it would have poured into the area. Construction started in the 1980s and blasting through bedrock, some fourteen miles of tunnels were hollowed out of the Texas earth.

However, through no fault of Dad, or Mick, or especially our cousin Jeff, the project was scrapped in 1993. Two billion dollars had already been spent, but there was competition for science money on other projects that seemed to have more merit. Estimates to finish the project had ballooned as high as $12 billion. Physicists from the US lamented the death of the Supercollider as a colossal blow to US science and scientific funding.

Following the demise of the Texas Supercollider project, the Hadron Collider was constructed beneath the borders of France and Switzerland, with a circumference of a mere 17 miles. (Everything was to have been bigger in Texas!) Apparently, the Hadron Collider has been a technological mother lode of physics, giving scientists the opportunity to explore such topics as the origin of matter and the Higgs Boson particle, neither of which I can pretend to understand at all.

However, there is one thing I am sure of: it hasn't made a hamburger.

Yet.

Disclaimer: After writing this story and doing a little research on the Supercollider, I realized the dates didn't correlate. Mom and Dad's anniversary party was held in the summer of 2000; the Supercollider project was scrapped in the early 90s. So how could Mick have told this story in 2000, as if the project were ongoing? I do not know.

Memories and memoir writing are, of course, subjective. Of this I am sure: Dad was frustrated in trying to understand the Supercollider and Mick was equally frustrated trying to explain it. Dad DID ask him if it could make a hamburger. I have a strong image of Dad sitting in the early evening sun in the driveway, hunched in a folding chair, rubbing his chin as he asked these questions. I know this conversation occurred after a family gathering and I felt certain it was after their 50th wedding anniversary celebration.

The Honest Woodsman
Dad, as a young boy, far right

The Honest Woodsman

"Once upon a time, there was a poor woodsman who lived in a forest with his family," Dad would begin his favorite story.

"One day he was out in the forest, chopping wood with his only ax, an old worn ax with a wooden handle. This was how he made money for his family. He was near a lake that day and as he chopped, suddenly he lost his grip on his ax and it flew from his hands. It fell with a splash into the lake and he could not see it.

The honest woodsman was very sad. He didn't have another ax and he didn't know how he was going to feed his family. He sat down on the bank of the pond and cried.

Suddenly a fairy appeared out of the water. She was holding a beautiful silver ax.

"Is this your ax?" she asked the woodsman.

The woodsman eyed the beautiful ax and knew that he could sell it and have a lot of money for his family. But he knew it wasn't his.

"No, it is not my ax," he answered honestly.

The fairy disappeared beneath the water. She reappeared a second time, holding a golden ax above her head.

"Is this your ax?" she asked.

"No, it is not my ax," he said sadly. "My ax is old and worn."

The fairy disappeared beneath the surface of the water. This time she reappeared holding an old worn ax.

"Is this your ax?" she asked a third time.

"Yes, yes!" the woodsman cried excitedly. "That is my ax!"

"You may have it," said the fairy and gave it to the woodsman. "But you may have the other two as well. Your honesty is rewarded."

Now there was also in the woods at that time, a dishonest man who had seen what had happened to the honest woodsman. Thinking that he also could get a gold and silver ax from the fairy, too, he purposely threw his own ax in the water.

Sure enough, the good fairy returned above the surface of the lake.

"Is this your ax?" she asked, holding a beautiful silver ax above her head.

"Yes, yes! That is my ax!" cried the dishonest man.

"You know it is not your ax," said the fairy. "Because you have been dishonest, you may not have this ax, nor the one you threw into the lake. You have been punished for your dishonesty.""

When Dad told us this story, we had no idea that this tale was very old, perhaps as old as six centuries B.C. and is considered to be one of Aesop's fables. We did not know who Aesop was – or consider the fact that Aesop himself may have been invented. We thought Dad himself had made up the Honest Woodsman story to drive home his all-encompassing life message: IN ALL THINGS, ALWAYS, ALWAYS BE HONEST.

Dad's view of honesty extended beyond just plain TELLING the truth; his view of honesty was BEING the truth – the truth of who you are. It was tied up in character and carefully considered principle: of keeping promises, of paying bills on time, of being a faithful husband and a present father, of giving his full attention to the work of being a good farmer – as best as he knew how.

So, identified with this intention of integrity, he became furious when something happened that challenged this essence of him, of being the Bill Bird that he strove to be.

A few incidents come to mind.

****

The creators of Craigslist may have thought they invented the idea of re-purposing, but farmers in our area frequently bought and sold equipment and livestock from each other. Without the advantage of the internet, they might listen to the swap and buy program on the local radio or hear by word of mouth that there was a welding machine, pickup tires, a set of ratchet wrenches, or as in Dad's case – a milk cow -to buy.

Milk was an important commodity in our house, served at every meal. If you do the math and multiply ten times three (people times glasses), you see that we needed about two gallons of milk a day. Allowing for the facts that we regularly drank more than one cup at a meal – especially if dessert was warm oatmeal or chocolate chip cookies – and that there was often a baby in the house, who subsisted only on milk (mixed with Karo syrup!), milk was a staple that we could hardly keep in supply. Sometimes we went through it so fast that we supplemented it with powdered milk ("As long as it's cold, you won't know the difference") or even had a milkman deliver it in glass bottles left by our door or inside the porch. But almost always there was an able-bodied Holstein in the barn, quietly chewing her cud and manufacturing milk – waiting for Dad or the boys to milk her twice a day.

Typically, a cow is not bred until she is a little over a year old, and just like humans, a cow cannot produce milk until she has given birth. And once she has done that, she will continue producing milk for perhaps two to five years (maybe longer, depends on the cow), as long as someone empties her udder regularly. Yet sometimes a cow will go dry (stop producing milk) without explanation.

So Dad bought a dairy cow from a farmer in the area, someone he did not know that well. I am not sure what he paid for her, but for some reason $200 sticks in my head.

Unfortunately, when Dad tried to milk the cow, he learned she was dry. He could not fathom how someone could be so deceitful as to sell a dry cow and he was livid. Dad knew this wouldn't be an easy situation to resolve, but he was determined that he should not be taken advantage of. He went to the farmer's house and told him he wasn't leaving until both the cow and the money went back to their rightful owners.

It took some doing – apparently Dad either stayed in his car or the farmer's house until the farmer capitulated- but eventually Dad left with his $200...and gave back one dry cow.

****

Dad and Mom were careful stewards of their money (see the essay on Frugality), working as tenant farmers of the Steele State Bank in Cherokee for over 25 years. Their agreement with the bank was 50-50; they and the bank split both profits and expenses down the middle. The only way to survive this arrangement and raise a family on our 320-acre farm was to watch every penny, paying close attention that the cost of growing grain would not outpace the profits from the yields.

Apparently, Dad was able to do this well enough that he caught the bank's attention. When the U.S. began selling corn to Russia for the first time in the 1970s, the demand for corn skyrocketed. Fueled by this need, farmers strove to produce more and more corn, realized large profits, and in many cases, began to buy more land. Noticing this trend, the bank approached Dad: would he consider becoming a farm loan officer at the bank – guiding farmers as they took out mortgages to buy land?

It was an unexpected offer and a nod to Dad's fiscal smarts. I remember him agonizing over this decision. He knew that taking the full-time job at the bank would put more responsibility on Mom and the boys, especially Tom and Jeff, for he would not be giving up the farm. They would have to do much of the work on the farm while he was at the bank. He would be juggling two occupations: farmer and loan officer and want to do his best at both. He knew that his presence at home would be very limited and this worried him more than anything else. Was it fair for mom to have to discipline the kids herself, especially the boys? (Tom and Jeff were teenagers and Dad worried that his fatherly influence would be missing at a critical time). Was it right for him to be away from home so much and then to expect our respect when he "dropped in" at the end of the day for supper? If he took this job and something went awry with one of us, he would never be able to re-do this decision. Yet despite all this soul searching, he decided this was an opportunity he couldn't pass up and took the loan officer job, with reservations.

As he had feared, it WAS difficult for mom to manage the farm and kids, although if anyone could have done it, it would have been her. The boys pitched in, Dad worked on the farm after his bank job, and the family muddled through this new situation as best they could.

Sometime after Dad had been in his bank job less than a year, he stopped at Snyder's Tap in town for a beer. In the bar, there was a local man, well known to Dad, who was drunk, as was frequently the case. Johnny (name changed) was clever and good with words and let his liquor talk that day.

"So you're a big banker now!" he said to Dad and puffed out his chest in imitation of a self-important rooster. "A b-i-i-g-g banker!" he drew out the words.

I wasn't there, but as the story goes, the man wasn't letting up until he got a reaction from Dad.

"Bill Bird's a big banker now!" he announced to the bar. "He's too good for the farm! He's working at the Steele State Bank! He's a big shot now!" The guy continued in that vein, egging Dad on, probably unaware that he was striking a very sensitive chord. Finally, Dad simply couldn't take it.

"Johnny," he said, "I want you to take a ride with me." If Johnny protested, Dad wasn't having any of it. "Get in my car," he said and grabbed Johnny by the arm.

I'm not sure how much resistance Johnny put up, but no matter, when Dad was angry, you didn't cross him: he would have his way.

Dad threw Johnny in the front seat of his car and drove six and a half miles out to our farm. He called all the kids who were home into the house and made them sit around the dining room table.

By this time, Johnny was getting more and more sober.

"Bill," he said, "I'm sorry. I was just having a little fun with you. Really, Bill, no harm done, right?"

"I want you to tell my kids what you told everybody in town," Dad said. "Tell 'em!"

"I'm sorry, Bill," Johnny said. "I didn't mean anything by it."

"Tell them," Dad said. "Tell them what a big shot I am."

I'm not sure how long this went on, but Dad was fierce and relentless when his integrity was challenged. He didn't back down and eventually Johnny had to repeat his insults. The kids listened in silence.

"All right, then Johnny," Dad said evenly when the confession was over. He led Johnny to the door, kicked him in the butt, and said:

"Now get on back to town."

No one knows if Johnny walked the whole six and a half miles back to town, or if he hitched a ride part way.

But the weather was mild and Dad didn't care; Johnny would make it back to Marcus and back to the bar.

At the end of this story, two facts remain.

Johnny never taunted Dad again.

And soon after, Dad left his job at the bank. Beset with misgivings, perhaps in small part pricked by Johnny's slings, he became a full-time farmer again.

****

Another honor story also has to do with Dad and money. Somehow, someone in the area was able to write a check from Dad's account and get a small amount of cash. Naturally, when Dad discovered this, he was very upset. Figuring that this person would try his forgery luck again in Marcus, Dad went to the local businesses and told them not to cash any checks from his own account.

The employee at Snyder's Tap – it wasn't Uncle Bud, who owned the bar – was most accommodating of Dad's wishes. So accommodating in fact that he posted a sign in full view of any patrons:

"DO NOT CASH ANY CHECKS FROM BILL BIRD."

Imagine Dad's humiliation when he stopped at the tap a few days later. To someone who made it his life's work to be honest and true, this was an insult of gargantuan proportion: a public announcement that his checks weren't good.

"Take down that sign!" I'm sure he demanded in a not-too-friendly tone.

To my knowledge, the check-cashing culprit was never identified and therefore never punished. Perhaps he is still lying low, afraid the ghost of Dad may somehow yet ferret him out.

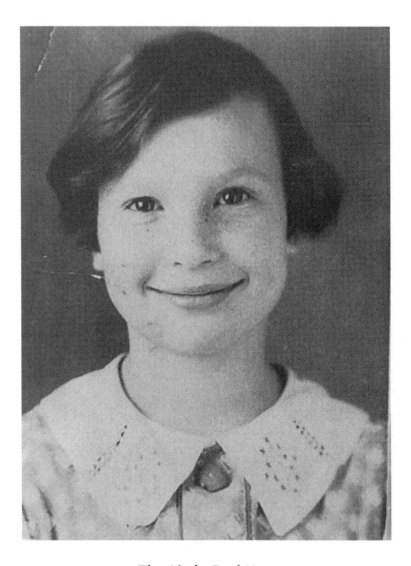

The Little Red Hen
Mom, as a bright young girl

The Little Red Hen

If the Honest Woodsman was Dad's signature story, perhaps Mom's story could have been the story of the Little Red Hen. If you remember, the Little Red Hen busied herself by walking around the farmyard ensuring all was tidy. One day in her meanderings, she discovered a pile of wheat seeds that had been spilt by the farmer. This gave her the idea to grow the seeds, raise some wheat, and make bread. She went around the barnyard, asking all the animals to help her: plant the seeds, harvest the wheat, grind the wheat, and make the bread. Not one of them— not the lazy pig wallowing in the mud, not the dreamy cat taking a nap, nor the duck cooling off in the pond – would help her.

No matter, the little red hen was quite capable herself. She went right ahead and took care of the wheat, made the bread, and ate it herself when the animals asked for a bite.

While Mom almost never asked for help beyond her kids and did share her bread with us, much about this little red hen embodied mom herself. She was tidy, industrious, and enterprising, with a can-do attitude that knew no limits. She would tackle any challenge and wrestle it into submission, and even if not perfect – it would be done, leaving her free to pursue the next project in line.

Much of mom's work had to do with simply keeping us fed and one of her biggest endeavors was taking care of her garden. If the weather permitted, she would start as early as St. Joseph's Day (March 19th) by planting potatoes. Cool weather plants would follow: lettuce, radishes, onions, beets, and carrots. Next were seeds that would erupt near the end of May (after the last frost): watermelon, cantaloupes, pumpkins, cucumbers, green beans, peas, and dill. Lastly, around Memorial Day, tender plants of tomatoes could be tucked in the finally warmed soil.

But planting the garden was just the beginning. Mom worked in it multiple times a week: thinning out shoots of radish and lettuce, pinching off tomato suckers and securing the vines to stakes with repurposed rages, picking the fruits of her labor, and showing us how to do it all. She would hoe with ferocity and energy that none of us kids working beside her could match: the blade cutting through the crust of gray black soil in efficient rhythmic strokes. When other farm women came to visit, especially her own mother, mom would often take them to the garden to show them her handiwork, tangible evidence of what she had been doing.

Once the vegetables were ready to be harvested, more work was in store, for nearly everything was canned. Mom was so adept at this, that for most crops she canned as she made bread – as part of the daily fabric of being a farm wife. When extra green beans were picked, she simply rustled up some Ball jars from the basemen, packed the beans in the hot, clean jars, threw in a little salt, wiped down the rims, placed the lid on the jar, screwed down the band, and processed them in the pressure cooker for 20 minutes. Following the same procedure, she canned tomatoes, beets, and pickles as they became ready.

But canning corn was a different matter. Sweet corn tended to become ready all at once and the processing was a family affair. Dad would pick four or five gunnysacks of corn the evening before, so that as soon as we had our breakfast the next morning, we took up our stations. Everyone had a job. Two or three of us sat in the back of the pickup, shucked the corn, and passed it on to one or two of the younger ones who would try to pick out any leftover corn silk. Two more kids would brush the ears to clean them. Next Mom would cut the kernels from the cob into a big enamel pan, the corn spattering her black glasses as she worked. Finally, the corn would be packed in jars (already washed in hot soapy water the night before) and processed in the pressure cooker.

Despite all the food prep work Mom HAD to do, she still had energy to experiment. Would it be possible to grow peanuts in Iowa? (Not much of a yield she found out; the growing season was too short.) Why couldn't she make her own ketchup with the abundance of tomatoes? (Nope, the homemade natural version lacked the punch of the stuff from a jar.) How could she use up all those cabbages? What about making sauerkraut?

THAT experiment turned out to be a success. From somewhere she conjured up a giant piece of crockery, shredded head after head of cabbage into it, doused it with canning salt, mashed it down with our smallest Louisville slugger, covered it with a dishtowel and a weighted board, then let it sit for a week or ten days in the basement. Periodically, she would peek under the towel and mash the cabbage a bit more, creating natural brine. When the sauerkraut was done, she packed that up in Bell jars, too, arranging it on shelves that lined the basement fruit room, along with the red tomatoes, green beans, and the yellow corn.

Despite the bounty of her garden – or perhaps on an off year - Mom sometimes had to supplement our meals. But she didn't simply hop in the station wagon, drive to town, and a pick up a couple cans of corn. She planned ahead and trekked 60 miles to a Storm Lake cannery and bought cans of dented peas, corn, and green beans – by the case. We girls made countless batches of cookies and brownies, but we often had "Johnson cookies" on hand - large boxes of broken and rejected cookies that Mom picked up cheap from a bakery in Sioux City.

And like the Little Red Hen making use of fallow wheat seeds, mom herself foraged...for apples. We didn't plant our own apple trees for years (perhaps thinking that we might move to our own land in the future?), but Mom knew that some people simply had more apples than they knew what to do with. So in late summer, just before school started, she would load a few kids and boxes in the station wagon and we would drive north through the countryside – where we no one knew us - looking for trees with apples on the ground. As we got older, we would cringe in the car while mom knocked on the farmhouse doors and explained that she had noticed unused apples on the ground. Would they mind if we picked them up so they didn't go to waste? If that were fine, she'd continue, were they going to use the ones on the tree? Sometimes the farm wife would ask us for a little money, but usually not. Once home, mom would core and stew the apples; we girls would spoon the soft hot fruit into a food mill, turning the handle to mash the pulp through the small holes in the strainer until all that was left was the paper-thin skins. Using this search and find method, we would scavenge up enough apples to can about a hundred jars of applesauce a year.

Mom made so much bread that it became second nature to her – and us. We thought nothing of seeing warm nutty wheat loaves cooling on racks twice a week, their dark bronze crusts glistening with a thin layer of margarine: they had just appeared. As if timing the mixing, kneading, raising, and baking of bread to fit in between loads of wash, ironing, cleaning, and disciplining kids wasn't enough for Mom, she added another layer: why not grind her own wheat? Shades of the Little Red Hen, she ordered her own cast iron grain grinder and took her bread making to another level. Experimenting with different proportions of white flour (needed to hold the dough together), wheat flour, and actual hand ground wheat kernels; she produced bread that was so delicious that it won "Best in Class" over all the baked goods at the Marcus Fair.

Mondays and Thursdays were always, always devoted to laundry – the only notable exception being Christmas and Thanksgiving. On laundry days immediately after breakfast, mom and one of us girls descended into the dank and musty basement, filled the Maytag washer with piping hot water, and threw in a cup of Tide to start the ten or so loads of laundry we'd produced in a few days. We flipped a lever to agitate the drum and tossed our white dishtowels into the soapy virgin water. When ten minutes or so had passed, we stopped the machine, fished out the dishtowels with a wooden wash stick and fed them through a wringer that squeezed out all but a few molecules of water. ("Watch your fingers!" Mom would periodically warn and then show us how to loosen the wringer – just in case.) The dishtowels would be rinsed twice in galvanized tubs – and through the wringer twice again - then finally hung outside to dry.

All the laundry was processed in the same way, following a prescribed and logical order with that allowed for both color and grime: whites sheets, white underwear and socks, colored shirts, white diapers, towels, colored socks, jeans and blue denim work shirts, coveralls, and finally throw rugs. Draining the water at the end also required cleaning out the bottom of the tub, which by that time was covered with a film of soil – as so much dirt had been extracted from our laundry.

Mom passed this laundry chore on to Jane and me as soon as she thought we were able. But the washing and the hanging outside and the bringing back in of the laundry was only the half of it. Not one piece of clothing was folded or put away if Mom saw it needed repair. Midafternoon on laundry day, she clacked away on her Sears machine - patching blue jean knees and reinforcing seams that had pulled apart. Socks with toe holes were mended over a dead light bulb, which she kept in a tin of orphaned buttons. Next, she tackled ironing our few good clothes and dad's blue work shirts, multi-tasking as best she could while listening to a book being read on the radio. (I clearly remember her listening to <u>Giants in the Earth</u> by Ole Rolvaag, a homesteading saga about the hardships Norwegian immigrants faced in the harsh climate of South Dakota.)

With eight of us just nine years apart living in a small three to four-bedroom house, Mom was constantly trying to keep order. One by one, when we went off to school and began bringing home books and papers, Mom wasn't flummoxed. This was just a problem to be solved. So long before backpacks came on the scene, she sewed book bags out of vinyl, designing a pattern with handles and a sturdy utilitarian zipper. I remember being slightly embarrassed with this homemade creation, but still I dutifully crammed all my school stuff in my off-white vinyl bag.

Mom had worked hard to get her nursing license at St. Joe's Hospital in Sioux City before we were born. She was only able to practice nursing for a short time before she married and had me. Yet, she never gave up the hope that someday she might go back to work and consequently through all the raising of kids, she made sure she kept up her CEUs – and thus, her license. Year after year, she subscribed to a nursing magazine, reading about new medications and procedures almost to the end of her life. Even when Dad was ill she did a home study course on caring for the elderly patient – both satisfying her CEU requirements and educating herself about taking care of Dad.

Mom's obligatory chores began to slow down as we grew up and left home. When she and Dad moved into town, Mom created a sewing center for herself in the basement and busied herself sewing more. One year for Easter, she made each family a floppy eared rabbit dressed in calico. When Marcus celebrated the sesquicentennial of its founding, we all returned home for the festivities, which included a parade. Somewhere there is a photo of the grandchildren watching the parade from Mom and Dad's lawn, all the girls clad in long "prairie dresses" which Mom had sewn on the same Sears machine. A few years after that she made quilts for the more than 20 grandchildren, each one identified with their name, year, and the words "From Grandma Bird" to remind them each of her.

When she and Dad visited us as adults, she brought her indefatigable energy with her. If it was the Christmas season, she'd untangle the lights for the tree and painstakingly go through the string, substituting bulbs until she found the ornery one that had caused the whole series to go dead. (I would have bought a new string!) She'd help decorate the house and trim the tree. She'd make cookies with the girls. She'd throw in laundry, fold it, put it away. She'd pick up the kids from school, help them with their homework, and then play cards with them. In our case, as we had a small farm, she would get under the sprayer with my husband to see why a nozzle was clogged. On her own, she took a gun case to the shoemaker to restitch the handle. Once within an hour of her arrival, she was fixing a leak under my kitchen sink. ("Kathy, get me a monkey wrench. Bill, go up to the hardware store and get some of that silicone lube.")

I'd knock myself out preparing for her arrival, taking care of loose ends and getting a little more prepared for each visit. Yet, if I finally got her to sit for a cup of coffee, she was restless.

"Say, where is that shirt of Mike's that needed a button?" she'd say. "If you get it for me, I'll fix it."

****

If all this industriousness was taxing when Mom visited, there was a time - when my children were born – that it was absolutely heaven sent. Except for the birth of Michael, my oldest, (when she still had Pat at home), Mom simply appeared, on her own or with Dad, to help. After Katie's birth, I remember waking in our Army housing duplex to the smell of both coffee and Lysol - and feeling so grateful that Mom was there. When I went into labor with Laura, mom and dad jumped in the car and drove for two days, arriving just after I came home with our new baby. As always, she made meals and did laundry while I tried to rest and nurse Laura. ("Kathy, do you have any of that Easy Off oven cleaner?") When Ryan was born in November 1989, again she and dad made the trek by car from Iowa. They stayed for a week and besides taking care of the usual chores, they immersed themselves in the preparation for the holidays, even to the point of helping Mike sell Christmas trees from our small farm. The night before they were to leave – in a rare moment of reflection – we sat with mom and dad, talking about our kids (now four of them!) and their activities, Mom and Dad's plans for Christmas, and the projected weather for their drive home.

"It's been a good visit and you have a beautiful baby boy," they said, summing up the past week. "We'll have a cup of coffee with you in the morning and say good-bye then."

Exhausted, I slept hard that night until I heard the baby cry about four a.m.

"Sh-sh-sh," I said, cradling Ryan so he wouldn't wake mom and dad. I walked into the hall, knowing the motion would soothe and quiet him, and then noticed mom and dad's room was empty.

A spurt of panic shot through me.

They were gone.

I held the baby closer, and then wiped a few of my own tears away with his blanket.

"Good-bye," I whispered to the red taillights disappearing down the driveway. "Good-bye." Disliking farewells, Mom and Dad had barely escaped this one.

"And thank you," I said into the silent dark night.

I rocked back and forth, patting Ryan's back. Then I sat on the window seat, preparing to nurse him, staying as close as I could to the last of Mom and Dad.

"Thank you," I said again as I touched my baby's week-old face. "Thank you."

Dad's Mid-Life Crisis

Today, when some men reach their forties, they buy Harleys or red convertibles. They invest in hair plugs. They take pilot lessons or long road trips. They leave their wives for younger women, or their corporate jobs to find themselves.

But these weren't options that a typical Iowa farmer considered in the late 1960s, least of all, Dad. Instead, when he turned forty, he embarked on a self-improvement program that involved not only him – but us, his eight children - as well.

I'm not sure where the idea came from. Perhaps during his endless hours alone on the John Deere – disking, plowing, planting, and cultivating his crops – he began thinking that he ought to challenge himself more. Perhaps he remembered that an officer in the Marines had once noticed his athletic ability and offered him a chance to play basketball at a university in Boston, but that he had thrown it away – along with the books he tossed in the Pacific Ocean. Perhaps one cold November while driving the corn picker through the dry stalks at harvest, trying to beat out a blizzard as dusk drew on, he decided that he ought to do something to break up the winter.

All I know is that one day, without any warning whatsoever to us, suddenly dad was going to become a public speaker. He enrolled himself in a Toastmaster's Club and started working on speeches. He gave informative speeches, humorous speeches, speeches with various voice inflections, speeches that used body motions, persuasive speeches, and inspirational speeches.

Why do I remember this so vividly? Because each week without fail, Dad had each of us do the same kind of speech he had just worked on. And we had to present in front of the toughest audience possible: our own brothers and sisters.

On Thursday night Dad would gather the ten of us together in our living room: four kids were crammed on the coffee colored couch, four others lay about on the dark beige carpet, and mom sat on the straight backed stuffed chair that she had reupholstered in tan, or some other shade of brown. Dad – in his blue work shirt and jeans, but freshly showered and shaved for the occasion - would start the family Toastmaster meeting off himself – welcoming us to our own living room as he stood in front of our small black and white TV. Standing there, reminding us of the type of speech that we were to give that night to our very own brothers and sisters, Dad looked ten feet tall, not six.

Following right on the heels of his classes, Dad made us all give informative speeches, humorous speeches, and persuasive speeches, too (with the overarching dictum not to us the word "um"). However, the absolute worst assignment was the speech that was designed to help us express our emotions.

The previous week, in order to get us primed, dad had told us to think of something that made us very angry. Then using that anger as a stimulus, we were to prepare a speech that showcased the intensity of our feelings.

We buzzed around the whole week. Something that made us angry? Did Dad actually want us to admit that we got angry and then on top of it – tell him about it in a speech? Gosh, up until this point, we hadn't been allowed to complain about anything EVER and now this?

We couldn't think of anything that would be safe to talk about.

Too many chores? Nah – that wouldn't go over very well.

Mom yelling at us? Nope – that could easily backfire.

Bad teachers? Shut your mouth and just do your work, Mom and Dad would say.

On the express-your-anger speech night, Dad told us all to roll up a piece of newspaper tightly before calling our Toastmaster meeting to order. He wrote each of our names on slips of paper and drew them out of a speckled melamine bowl, one by one, assigning the order of our speeches. He moved a dining room chair next to the imaginary podium in front of the TV.

"What you're going to do when you do your talk," he said, with a serious expression in his blue eyes, and rubbing his chin, "is take this newspaper and hit it on the chair when you get mad in your speech. It will help you express yourself."

I have no idea what safe anger topic I or anyone else talked about. I do remember starting out with a sheepish feeling and thumping the Sioux City Journal half-heartedly on the chair. I didn't make eye contact with my audience – my brothers and sisters - and I didn't pause here and there for emphasis. But oddly, as I talked, my voice rose to a crescendo and I beat the paper into shreds before the embarrassment of the situation got to me and I ended my speech in tears, as did most of my brothers and sisters.

Somehow, we got through that night. Dad went on to win prizes in Toastmaster competitions with his humorous speech about his Marine Corps basic training (how could that be humorous?), wearing his twenty-year-old uniform. He finished the "Competent Communicator" series of entry-level Toastmaster speeches and we finished our hand-me-down lessons right along with him.

We breathed a sigh of relief when it was all over. We hoped to go back to our normal Thursday nights: playing cards or Monopoly or reading or even fighting, for Pete's sake. No more speeches to our brothers and sisters, trying to not to use the word "um" and remembering to speak in clear, distinct voices.

But no, dad was on a roll. Someone in Toastmaster's had introduced him to Dale Carnegie's book, "How to Win Friends and Influence People."

"It's a course, too," he told us. "I start next week and I'll teach it to you."

Frugality

"1953 – Income and Expense"

Frugality

Not too long before she died, Mom handed me a slim brown spiral composition book.

"You might be interested in this," she said. "I saved it and I'm giving each of you kids the records from the year you were born."

In Dad's handwriting on a narrow strip of paper, yellowed by time and the Scotch tape that covered it, were the words: "1953 – Income and Expense." I thanked Mom, put the book away, and revisited it thoroughly for the first time just recently. I had known, of course, that mom and dad were thrifty, but a careful perusal of their financial records is a window into their life as a young farm couple as well.

The first page, identified in faint pencil as "Jan Expense 1953," begins the story of their life on a 320 corn and soybean farm. Listed simply, line by line are the expenses they incurred:

"1. Evans Clothing Co – work clothes and 5 buckle overshoes $7.25"

"2. Harry Erickson – trucking $2.31"

"3. Wheel weights and spacers and repairs $4.25"

January 1953's expenses go on to include 31 items, the majority of which are farm related, such as "Dr. Nelson – penicillin cow's udder - $4," "Elwood Green – shelling 100 bu. corn - $2.50," and even "Gerald Meylor – ½ of spot boar - $15.00" (apparently an arrangement with a neighbor to share the services of a boar).

About a third of the items, while legible, have a firm line drawn through them. It took little sleuthing to figure out that these items, while noting money spent, were not applicable to taxes. For example, "Anniversary second - $5" is crossed out as well as six or so entries with amounts ranging from 15 cents to one dollar and twenty cents spent on "peanuts, pop, potato chips, candy bars, and coffee," etc. The accounts book served as sort of a self-censure for Dad, too. Entry #27 shows that he spent 50 cents on 2 bottles of beer but was remorseful enough to write: "A fool and his money are soon parted" above it. Later in the month, he played euchre for money and apparently lost. "Foolishness" he wrote on the same line where he recorded the dollar it cost him.

January 1953 was not such a good month financially for mom and dad. Most of the $283.33 they earned came from the sale of eggs. The price per dozen varied a bit from 34 to 38 cents a dozen and their biggest take was $42.56 from selling 112 dozen eggs to "Sheehan LeMars." Their simple, but effective, accounting showed that they spent $607.48 in farm expenses and $64.18 on non-tax related items, with a farm income loss of $324.15 for the month.

In February, they fared better, selling 28 head of cattle for $6201.21. Still it took an unquantifiable amount of labor to keep livestock, not to mention the feed it required to raise them. It was difficult to know whether raising chickens (for eggs), cattle (for beef), cows (for milk), and pigs (for pork) was profitable and worth Dad's time. At the end of the February income sheet, he mused on each of these livestock:

"Remarks. Chickens. 2 died during Feb. posted* one- leucosis. Did not post (*have the vet test the dead animal for disease) second one. Chickens ate 20# oats, 14# corn, 13# protein per day. Av. Feed cost per day for 215 chickens housed - $1.62 – my share $1.16." …. "Production good. 65% x 215= 140 eggs per day. 140 @ .03 each = $4.20 - $1.16= $3.04 per day."

"Cattle – did a poor job of feeding them. They should have been fed ground ear corn. Did not like self-feeding corn. Cattle slobber on feed and lose some appetite. Cattle were well bedded and they like that."

"Cows do much better on ground oats then whole oats. Avoid having them lay in the cold. Checked some serious inflammation in one cow's udder by giving her good dry bed. Cows are and must be contented for maximum (milk) production. They waste some feed by moving their head away from over feed boxes."

"Sows. Almost afraid to figure out how much feed they eat. They really eat a lot. Feed should be ground and fed in feeder. Make extra effort to keep feed clean and bulky for sows. They should also have constant fresh clean water. Automatic waterer."

In summary, Dad resolved to continue figuring out the profit margin on livestock. "It does not pay just to <u>have</u> livestock around," he wrote. (Underlining is his emphasis.)

Their records for February of that year show the hospital cost for my birth was $40.32 and that Dad spent $2.50 for "food, calls, paper, etc." on the 14th and 15th awaiting my birth (Mom's labor in delivering me spanned two days.) Two months later in April, Dad paid Dr. Joynt $14.50 for the rest of my bill – "maternity." Apparently, that same month, mom was in the hospital herself: "Sacred Heart Hosp. Arlene tonsils Blue Cross paid $29.00 & we pd. $5."

Month after month, they dutifully recorded expenses and income, almost solely in Dad's handwriting. After January, they did not total expenses or income for the month, perhaps in part discouraged by the always longer list of expenses. It appears that they existed mostly on the sale of those 28 head of cattle and eggs (always around .38 a dozen) until June, when finally, there was another substantial entry.

"Farmer's Elevator," the last entry of the month reads, "540 bu. @ .67 less trucking 11.12." Records from the Iowa State Extension Service indeed show that the price of corn per bushel in June 1953 was $1.38, hence Dad's half tenant share of .67 per bushel, bringing his net gain for the corn sale to $350.87 (less the trucking expense.)

For our 320-acre farm – a half section – was owned by Steele State Bank, a family run bank in Cherokee, Iowa that had been in operation since 1874. Under their arrangement with the bank, Mom and Dad would split both expenses and earnings (at least for grain) with the bank, so only half of the sale price went to Mom and Dad. Consequently, good records were important not only for tax purposes, but for squaring up with the Steele State Bank also.

April 1953 Income

At the end of 1953, Dad listed his gross profit at $12, 953.94, less depreciation (of equipment) $1187.03, and less expenses of $9771.47. Thus for 1953, they ended up in the black by $1995.44.

Although Mom and Dad must have worried about finances, I never heard them talk about their lack of money in front of us. In fact, I don't remember much preaching about being good stewards of money. We got the sense that it was a bad thing to owe money. We understood that you should pay your bills immediately. We knew that you should put extra money in the bank and not spend all that you have. We saw that you should be watchful about your finances; that there were people who might sometimes try to cheat you and that you should speak up on your own behalf if you thought this was true. We saw that you should try to fix things (Dad in his toolshed – welding; Mom at the sewing machine – patching.) We saw that you should read about your occupation (*Wallace's Farmer, Nursing*) and be mindful of what might be changing in it (farm government regulations, grain prices, new medications, etc.)

We were aware that Mom and Dad did not own their farm and that they were beholden to their landowners, the bank. We understood from that arrangement that you should be respectful to your employers. It is perhaps to learn that lesson that Mom and Dad thought it important for us to have part time, sometimes onerous jobs, outside our home as we got older. We girls detasseled corn in the stifling heat of July and waitressed for $1 an hour at a local café. The boys worked on other farms baling hay – again on the hottest days of summer when the hay would be thoroughly dry, walking beans, and operating farm equipment. They shingled roofs and helped to build hog confinements on weekends. We were not expected to buy our own clothes or supply gas for the car that we shared as high schoolers, but instead expected to save the money we earned, which most of us obligingly did.

Harking to their practice of keeping an expense book, Mom would sometimes give this piece of advice: "Write everything down that you spend, that way you can see where the money goes." A simple bit of advice that proved oh-so-surprising when my husband and I used it early in our marriage. I wasn't spending five and ten cents on peanuts and candy bars, but $5 here or there for books that I could get at the library or soda I didn't even need. Keeping a log like this for just a few months showed us in black and white, that there were many ways we were wasting money.

In the end, Mom and Dad's frugality paid off immensely. The very bank that had owned their land for the first 35 years of their married life, a bank that had been in existence since northwest Iowa was first settled, a bank that had been managed by the same family for over one hundred years, a bank that had weathered the Great Depression, went under. Beset by "excessive loan losses" caused by the farm crisis of the 1980s, Steele State Bank was closed down by the Iowa Department of Banking on January 25, 1985.

Thus in 1986, after thirty-five years of paying close attention to their finances and slowly, but surely saving their money, Mom and Dad were finally able to buy the very farm they had rented their entire married life.

Leaving

Judy, the head waitress, leaned against the counter, tipped her head back and puffed lazy smoke rings through her full siren red lips. Her eyes were closed behind her thick-framed glasses; her copper hair teased and wound into a stiff French twist. Carl, the beefy and jovial town cop, sat on the last stool and smoked, too. He held his cigarette with thumb and forefinger tight against his mouth for a moment, eyes narrowed with the effect of inhaling, but I knew he was watching Judy. She knew it, too. She took another deep drag on her cigarette, cheeks sucking in hard, held in the smoke. He balanced his cigarette on the edge of the half-filled ashtray, removed his cap, placed it on the counter, and crossed his arms, ready to devote his full attention to Judy. Suddenly, she opened her heavily lined eyes, stood up straight, and exhaled through flaring nostrils. She crushed her cigarette out in Carl's ashtray and looked at me instead. Carl sat up with a jolt, the moment spoiled.

"So, what are you gonna do about that Army thing?" she demanded of me.

I felt the sealed envelope in the pocket of my uniform. It was April 24th, 1971 and the return letter in my pocket had to be postmarked that day. The Paullina post office - just across the street - closed at noon on Saturdays. I had two hours to decide.

"I don't know," I said, my hand on the almost weightless envelope. Inside was a document that I had carefully signed, forming each letter perfectly, aware of the momentous decision my signature would put into motion. I, Kathryne Ann Bird, did agree to enter the United States Army for a period of seven years under the Walter Reed Army Institute of Nursing Program. A simple document, that once mailed would entail a free college education, a commission in the Army Nurse Corps, and a chance to travel. I could go to college anywhere the first two years, then transfer to Walter Reed for the last two years (earning a BSN from the University of Maryland) and finally work three years as an Army nurse to pay back my education. The next seven years of my life would be completely laid out for me, planned in concrete detail. I had only to mail the very official paperwork.

"Why? What's the problem?" Judy said, lighting up again.

"For one thing, I'll be 25 when I finish it all," I said. "That's so old."

"My Jennifer was eight years old by the time I was twenty-five," said Judy. "I had to raise her all by myself, but I did it."

"Oh," I said. Was this a point for or against joining the Army?

"It's good to have your babies early," Judy continued, making it clear that she thought time was slipping away if I wanted to have kids. Judy seemed proud of her unwed mother status, something I couldn't understand. I looked at Carl, who was not the father of

Judy's Jennifer. He raised his eyebrows, put his policeman's cap back on, and stood up to go.

"And I guess you've thought about that war, too?" Judy asked, back to blowing smoke rings.

"Yeah," I said, but Vietnam seemed a surreal place that couldn't touch me in this tiny café where I made one dollar an hour and if I was lucky, an extra one or two dollars a day in tips. Vietnam, with its whirring choppers on the nightly news, its daily body counts, and the protests it spawned was far, far away. Besides, I reasoned (and luckily, I was right!), I'd be in college for four years and maybe by the time I finished school, just maybe, the war would be over. If I decided not to take the scholarship, Vietnam would not be the reason.

If I decided not to go, it would be because of words. I loved words and I couldn't get enough of them. I loved my high school composition classes and journaling and the kooky Mrs. Kloster, who read our journals and probably violated every privacy code in doing so. I loved World Lit and the slightly hunched librarian who taught it, whispering about the indiscretions of <u>Madame Bovary</u> to the eight of us girls who took her class. I loved diagramming and figuring out the parts of speech. I could do Chemistry and Geometry and Algebra, but I'd always come back to words. If I decided not to join the Army, it would be because I'd made up my mind to immerse myself somehow in the world of words: savoring them, devouring them, surrounding myself with them and maybe sharing my passion for words through teaching.

But everything's paid for with the Army, Mom's voice spoke to me from inside my head. Everything. And it's really hard to get a teaching job. What would you do if you graduated and couldn't find a job? You can always get a job in nursing and you can use it with a family. But you decide; it's up to you.

"Well?" said Judy. "You've only got a couple hours. What are you gonna do?"

I shrugged. "Is it okay if I go out for a minute? I think the coffee run's done and I've got the silverware wrapped for lunch."

Outside, I leaned against the glass storefront of Lange's Café. If I had smoked - like Judy - this would be a good moment for it. The sun was intense for April in Iowa and I squinted across the wide main street to Halverson's Grocery. Craig, the grocery boy, pushed through the door and held it open with his thick body for an older woman with tight gray curls and sensible shoes. He caught my eye, and arms full of grocery bags, acknowledged me with a quick lift of his chin. I waved and watched his white shirt stretch across his broad back as he loaded the groceries into the cavernous trunk of Mrs. Wainwright's Chevy. He glanced quickly down each side of the yawning street, and then jogged over to meet me, shoulders drawn up, arms held closely to his side, apron knotted at his waist.

"Hey," he said. "What are you doing out here?"

"Not much," I said. "I'm going to the post office. Wanna come?"

What the heck, I remember thinking, looking at the letter setting on the open lid of the post office box, hanging in the balance. I was tired of thinking about it. I was tired of wondering what the right choice was – nurse or teacher, Army or not. What if I mailed this letter, setting in motion the next seven years, and realized I didn't even like nursing? What if I didn't accept this scholarship, instead became an English teacher, and wasn't any good at it? And maybe, as Mom had warned, I wouldn't even be able to get a job. What then? There was no way I could ever go back home, admitting defeat.

I couldn't envision how either decision would play out. There were too many variables even beyond the career for which I would be educated. What kind of friends would I make in the Army? Would they be rigid and inflexible? What kind of friends would I make as an Iowa teacher? Would they – all being from the Midwest – be rigid and inflexible in a different way? What if the war in Vietnam didn't end before I graduated? I didn't like guns or violence. How would being committed to the military affect me? And what about traveling? As a teacher, I would most likely stay in Iowa; in the Army, I would see Washington, D.C. and beyond...

Was it the trips we had taken as kids? The far-off places depicted in the books we had carted home from the Marcus Public Library? A niggling desire to see more of the world, but a fear of making my own decisions to do just that?

Something tugged at me.

I could always write on the side.

I let the letter go.

I was going to be an Army nurse.

****

And so, two years later, after finishing my pre-nursing classes at Briar Cliff in Sioux City, the reality hit home. During my first two years in college, I had been receiving a private's wage, plus fully paid tuition, yet I had no uniform or military obligations on weekends. To everyone at Briar Cliff, I looked like any other college student with faded jeans and clogs, who sometimes wore a bandana when she hadn't washed her hair. But now, it was time to make the move to Walter Reed in Washington; it was time to officially identify myself with the Army. I had boxed up my meager belongings (winter clothes, a few books, and my Kenmore sewing machine), listed them on a bill of lading, and followed instructions to have them shipped to WRAIN (Walter Reed Army Institute of Nursing) courtesy of the Army.

Everyone was up by five that August morning that I left home – all seven of my siblings – as my plane was leaving mid-morning from Omaha, a good two and a half hours away. Mom was busy in the kitchen, frying pounds of bacon, toasting her homemade bread, and scrambling two dozen eggs. My boyfriend had come to join us and take me to the airport.

Seeing them all there, seated around the linoleum-covered table with the metal edging (a practical product of mom's), each of them in their usual seats, the significance of the Last Breakfast became all the more momentous. They were there to see me off and I was definitely leaving them all. I began to cry.

I remember wiping a few random tears away at first, then more and more, as my emotions got the better of me. I passed around the heaping platters as they came by and ate a bite of everything, because that's what I knew I should do, even though it was all tasteless to me. The talk rose and fell about me as if it were the most ordinary day in the world. When did Tom start classes at Vermillion (University of South Dakota)? Was Jane going to bring her new Nova to college for her sophomore year? The patch on the pickup's flat tire wasn't going to hold; Dad would need to get a new tire after all. It was Mary's turn to hoe the garden with Joe. Mom would be making applesauce later that day. Could someone pass the butter? Who wants that last piece of bacon?

I'm leaving! I wanted to call out. I'm going far, far away! I won't be able to get back here unless I get on a plane!

They tied up the last bits of conversation and we finished up our bacon and eggs. Still crying, I got in the car with my large green suitcase – part of a graduation set of luggage that signaled each of us that we would need to leave home. I wasn't just transferring colleges; I wasn't just going on to complete my education; I wasn't just temporarily going to live somewhere else. In a sense, I had made the decision to leave two years before, but in reality, I was making it then, in real time. I knew I was leaving Iowa forever.

From the car, I waved good-bye to my family, who had left the breakfast table and stood outside by the weathered fence. I would see them in a few short months for Thanksgiving and a month after that for Christmas. I would see them for spring breaks and summer vacations, for weddings and showers, for anniversaries and family reunions throughout the years. But something changed forever that day.

I had always been one of the Birds, one of eight, the oldest in a passel of kids. I had been nurtured and nourished; challenged and critiqued. I had been educated and prodded. I had witnessed faith and integrity first hand. I had learned to be industrious and responsible. And ultimately, I had been thoroughly loved by my parents.

It was time to become me.

Kathryne Bird Belby is a former Army nurse who also holds an MFA in Professional Writing from Western Connecticut University. She is the mother of four adult children and lives with her husband, Mike, in rural New Jersey. She believes the act of writing a memoir not only preserves family history but will bring about positive interior change to those who try it.

She thanks her husband, Mike, for his support of this project and her siblings for their approval of the content of this book. Special thanks go to her brother, Jeff, who prodded her to undertake and then continue writing family stories. She also thanks her sister, Jane, who provided technical advice on self-publishing.

In addition, she is grateful to the staff of the Western Connecticut MFA program, in particular to Brian Clements, Don Snyder, Paolo Corso, Tim Weed, Daniel Rose, Oscar De Los Santos, and James Lomuscio.

Made in the USA
Lexington, KY
01 July 2018